41 SIGNS of
Hope

Dave Kane

FIRST EDITION

Published by
New River Press
645 Fairmount Street
Woonsocket, R.I.02895
(800) 244-1257
www.newriverpress.com

Printed in the United States of America

ISBN-10 1-891724-05-3
ISBN-13 978-1-891724-05-3

Cover illustration by Charlie Hall

Nicholas O'Neill

Dedication
With love to Joanne,
without whom this book,
and Nicky, would not
have been possible.

Foreword

Robert Brown
International Medium

When Dave Kane asked me to be part of this book, I was deeply honored. I first met Dave and his wife, Joanne, through my work. I'm a medium, a person who, it's often said, speaks with the dead.

Dave and Joanne visited me for a consultation. When people come to see me, I usually have only their first names and an arrival time. From the start of the appointment, I tell everyone that I don't know what information, if any, will come through. Any reputable medium will not guarantee that the person you are seeking to contact will make a connection, and I tell people to run a mile from any medium who says that he or she can guarantee it. If mediums can categorically attest to being able to just get anyone they wish, then surely they are also saying that they have a hold over your loved ones. They do not. A medium merely has an ability.

There is so much more to a successful sitting....

The person who has passed must be ready and willing to communicate. There is no set or standard time frame for this; it's simply when they are ready. The sitters (those who seek the consultation with the medium) have to be open and objective, but they do not have to be believers. Often what they are coming for is to find some truth.

Most mediums work very hard and explain that they, too, only want to get to the truth, but they do not want sitters who are just going to agree with everything they say. I tell people that fixating on a loved one and trying to "will" them to connect with us is almost as bad for a sitting as a cynic who would deny anything you bring through. I ask people to invite their loved ones mentally, then just let the spirit that is part of all of us do the rest.

I need not have concerned myself with Dave Kane and his preparations. Dave had "done his homework." He had checked me out and taken every precaution that I did not know who he was or why he was here. He was on a mission: He wanted answers and was going to get them! So we had a medium willing to work, and Dave, a man on a mission! We had two parts of what it takes for a successful sitting.

What happened next astounded me, even after thirty-two years as a medium. When Dave and Joanne's teenaged son joined us from the spirit realms, I believe one of the things that I relayed was that Nick had been an "old soul in a young body." Never was that saying more appropriate!

During our time together, Nick projected images, words, symbols, names and even whole recollections of family events. These weren't just things that had happened while he was alive, but things that had taken place since his passing, the youngest victim of the terrible 2003 Station nightclub fire in Rhode Island. Nick wasn't shy when it came to getting his messages across, and it was abundantly clear that the love between him and his parents was the facilitator for our successful time together.

It was clear that Nick was exceptional, and had been throughout his short time on the Earth plane. Why was he going to be any different in his quest to show his parents his survival?

Many years ago, the great medium and prophet Edgar Cayce would make sure that all his readings were recorded. This I have always done also, these days using audio tapes. I can't think of one legitimate reason for any medium to forbid taping. If I hadn't taped the session with Dave, Joanne and Nick, we would have missed one of the most remarkable comments to have been relayed as evidence. Who would feel comfortable having sat with parents for an hour, hearing so much from their son, and hearing him say, "Tell my dad: The show must go on," and relaying that at such a poignant moment.

I found myself saying exactly what Dave, Joanne and I *knew:* that their clever, witty, bright, charming and incredibly spiritual son had shown us all something so important: Love is the password to heaven!

I will leave it to Dave to explain the importance of that most unusual sentence. Nick has not once but many, many times proved his existence and, lest any reader suspect that Dave and Joanne are "grasping at straws," you will see in this book just how many people have witnessed Nick's ability to make himself known. He has shown many of us that signs are not limited to flickering lights and the odd memory played on the radio. Nick's communications show intelligent thought, planning and a clear knowledge of the fact that those who experience his signs will *know* it is Nick. He is indeed an old soul in a young body, but then again, why are we surprised?

Don't we say: "As below, so above"?

I hope Dave's mission to find answers for himself and his family also helps others to seek their own truths. I'm grateful that I was allowed to play a small part in this. Every communication a medium has should help him or her to learn.

I thank Nick for what he has taught me!

Morlaix, France, 2005

Introduction:
The Beginning

Dave Kane

On February 20, 2003, we lost our eighteen year-old son, Nicholas O'Neill, in the fourth largest nightclub fire in United States history. The Station nightclub in West Warwick, Rhode Island, was totally engulfed in flames in just ten seconds because of indoor pyrotechnics, flammable materials and other factors. But this book is not about a fire. It's about the aftermath of a tragedy: A continuing echo of signs and spiritual "visits" that I hope you will find both comforting and uplifting.

Nick was an actor, a musician, a singer, a comedian, a composer, and a prolific writer. When he was just sixteen, Nick wrote a one-act play he called *They Walk Among Us.* This play is about teenagers who die and return as guardian angels. This wonderful work is not only prophetic but a moving and inspirational celebration of life and hope!

Since Nick's passing, his family and friends have experienced a myriad of unexplained signs and events, most of these connected with the number 41. These occurrences have not only helped comfort us, but have gone a long way to assure us that our loved ones never really die. They are still here, around us and with us at every moment of every day.

To many people, these stories will have a very familiar ring. They tell of happenings that at first seem impossible. Most people hesitate to share these tales with others. They worry that their stories

As a baby, Nick O'Neill already sports the number 41!

will be written off as nothing more than the imaginings of an aggrieved loved one. But I know better, and the time has come to share these wonders.

I hope this book will bring you comfort, encouragement and trust in a belief that there is something more, something to embrace with all your heart. My wish is that these writings will bring you hope!

Johnston, Rhode Island, 2005

41 SIGNS of HOPE

Publisher's Note

As this book was being prepared for publication, two different editors worked with the text, which was edited and arranged into chapters as it arrived. At no time was it planned in advance, either by the author or publisher, that the book contain 41 chapters. This was an apparent "coincidence" that occurred during the production process.

Paul F. Eno
President, New River Press

-1-
'Call My Father!'

We named him Nicholas, after the patron saint of children. St. Nicholas, Santa Claus. Of course, many children are named after saints. But we never realized just how special this choice was. It never occurred to us that our son, who displayed so much love and concern for others, especially children, would barely have made his first step into adulthood when he passed.

I say "passed" and not "died" because I don't believe that anyone ever really dies. They pass into an entirely new realm. One that I can't prove exists, but that I believe in more every day.

My friend Cindy Gilman is a talented singer who has traveled extensively and entertained audiences all over the country. But Cindy has another talent, one she has possessed from a very early age. Cindy is a spiritual medium.

I first heard of Cindy many years ago, when she hosted a very successful radio show. Every week she would take calls from people who were looking for information on a raft of subjects, but most wanted to know about loved ones who had passed. I would listen as callers, some with tears in their voices, would ask for something — anything — that would give them comfort and peace. Cindy would amaze me as she told these people things she couldn't possibly know.

Some years later I asked Cindy to be a guest on my own radio show. She jammed the lines with former listeners wanting to greet her and tell stories of her "on target" readings. And there were many calls from those who had never heard Cindy, hoping she could do the same for them. I really liked Cindy, and I had always been amazed at her ability and desire to bring hope and spiritual serenity to everyone she encountered. Little did I know that this loving, five-foot-tall woman, who was sitting in my studio giving messages to total strangers, would one day be the courier of a deeply personal message to me.

It was the morning of February 21, 2003. It was the morning after the disastrous Station nightclub fire in West Warwick, Rhode Island. I was in my car, going I don't know where, doing I don't know what. I did that a lot in the days that followed the fire.

I got a call on my beeper from Cindy. She left a message offering to help in any way she could. At first I wasn't going to return that call; I just didn't feel capable of carrying on a coherent conversation. But then I wondered how she had known about Nick, since the media hadn't even released the name of the victims yet. So I decided to call Cindy after all.

When she answered the phone, Cindy's first words were about how she wanted to help those who had lost family members and friends in the fire. She offered to be on my radio show. She told me that she wanted to reassure those who had lost loved ones. You see, Cindy believes, as I do, that those who have passed are still with us on a spiritual level and are not really gone at all.

I interrupted Cindy to tell her that we had lost our Nicky in that fire, and she couldn't believe it. I could hear the genuine shock in her voice!

"I knew it! I should have said something!"

When I heard those words, I felt instant fury. Tears came to my eyes. I couldn't believe she would say that to *me*! I told Cindy that I had to get off the phone, and I hung up.

I'm sure that my reaction confuses you; it certainly confused me.

You see, I never expected to hear Cindy say what she did. Like you, I over the years have been exposed to people who claimed to have the gifts that I believed Cindy truly possessed. Too many times I was disappointed. I would listen to these "wannabes" flounder around, ask question after question, search for clues, and miss the mark every time. They would say, "That's what I meant," or "I was going to say that!" Of course it wasn't what they were going to say at

So when I heard Cindy use a similar phrase, it shook my belief in someone I had respected very much.

As I look back, I realize that I was exhausted. I hadn't slept. I was in a complete fog and completely desperate. I have always believed that the secret to living life is in how we respond to it. My mother used to say that life is like a grinding wheel. We're either ground down or polished by it, depending on what we're made of.

Well, at that moment, I had no idea what I was "made of." My world was crashing down around me, and I couldn't do a damn thing about it.

The next morning, after I'd had a little sleep, I started to think about my conversation with Cindy. Although I was still upset, I thought I owed her an explanation for ending our call so abruptly. I called her and tried to explain why I'd been so upset. Her response, as usual, was very gracious. As a matter of fact, there was almost a smile in her voice.

You see, Cindy had an explanation for me too.

On the night of the fire, Cindy was awakened by a "vision" of what she described as a "charred" boy. This young man kept saying to Cindy, "Call my father! Call my father!" Needless to say, Cindy didn't know what to do with this. But the boy wouldn't leave her alone.

"Call my father!"

Finally, not knowing what else to do, Cindy opened her personal phone book at random. And there, she saw the name "Dave Kane." Cindy told me that seeing my name gave her an idea. Her plan was to come on my show, tell the story of her visitor and his insistence that she call his father. It was important for Cindy to try to make this connection.

As it turned out, of course, Cindy didn't need to go on the air at all. As soon as she heard what I told her during our conversation on the morning after the fire, she realized immediately that the young boy in her vision was Nick, and that his message was for me!

-2-
41 to Begin

My guess is that most people have a lucky number. We all seem to have a favorite series of digits that we use for bets and lotteries. These numbers might be your birth date or those of your children, your high school locker number, or the date you were married. Well whatever it is, these numbers are usually chosen for a special reason. Nick had a favorite number but, in his case, the number seemed to choose him.

From the time he was very young Nick had what I would describe as an odd connection with the number 41. For some reason he would notice this number everywhere. When he got in the car, he'd say, "Hey, Dad! Look, its 2:41." He was always spotting "41s." No matter where it was: license plates, house numbers, sales receipts, football jerseys, Nick would let us know.

For the longest time, we tried to figure out what this "41" thing was all about, but we could never come to any conclusion. Nick and his brother Chris would talk about the significance of 41, but they never came up with answers either. Now you might think that after Nick passed we would have forgotten about it. But in the days, weeks and months to follow, that ubiquitous number 41 seemed to take on a life of its own. At first, we looked at these "sightings" and appearances as coincidences. Then we began to realize that there was much more to this than coincidence.

Consider this: Nick lived to the age of eighteen years and twenty-three days. Those two numbers add up to 41. The Station nightclub was located at latitude 41.41. The number of the fire call box at The Station site was 4414, and the company that made the soundproofing foam that got much of the blame for the fire's quick spread was founded in 1941. But the most interesting of these connections to the number 41 pre-dates all of these.

Joanne's Uncle Paulie had been looking at some home videos. You know the stuff: birthday parties, cookouts, vacation films and the like. As Paulie watched these memories flickering on the screen, he suddenly saw something that had him rubbing his eyes. It was in some footage of Joanne at her mother's house during a family gathering. She was holding Nicky, who couldn't have been more than a year old at the time. Nicky was dressed in a baby outfit made to look like a baseball uniform. The number on the ballcap was 41.

With these facts in mind and the many unexplained events and stories you're about to read, I've come to believe that there is no such thing as coincidence. Nothing is happenstance, and there is no such thing as accident. On some level these events have a purpose. We may not understand them now, but that doesn't mean we won't some day and soon.

-3-
The Elks Sign

My mother used to say that shock is a wonderful thing. She felt that there was a kind of foggy cocoon that encased those who had suffered serious physical or emotional wounds. She thought of it as a protective "bubble" that allowed people to appear to function normally even in the face of life's most devastating events.

On February 22, 2003, just two days after the fire, the one-man dinner-theater show that I do, entitled *Misgivings*, had been booked at an Elks Lodge in Pawtucket, Rhode Island. Anyone, including myself, would have expected me to cancel that show, and frankly that's just what I planned to do. I couldn't imagine walking on stage and expecting my audience to ignore the dagger of sorrow protruding from my chest.

I simply could have picked up the phone and cancelled. After all, this was the worst fire Rhode Island had ever seen, and virtually everyone in this small state had been touched in one way or another by the tragedy. Certainly no one would blame me for simply rescheduling. But the more I thought about pulling out of the show, the more I thought about Nick.

Nick was a dedicated performer. He was singer, a composer, an actor, a musician, a comedian and a playwright. Totally at home on stage, he had many talents, and he just loved sharing them. I knew what Nick would want. I decided to do the show.

Misgivings is an evening with an Irish Catholic priest, Fr. Patrick Aloysius Misgivings. There is a collection, a raffle, and even a real bingo game. It's eclectic and interactive. But when I wrote the show I felt an obligation to do more than just make it funny. I wanted the audience to leave the show feeling good, not only about themselves but about their relationship with God.

I got to the Elks Hall around 10 a.m. that Saturday. I had to bring in my equipment and set up the staging area. That done, I began running through every detail of the show in my mind, over and over. I was very tense.

During the show there's a segment in which Fr. Misgivings talks about death. He chides those present for being afraid to die. Then he attempts to comfort the audience by telling them there's no reason to be afraid. At the close of this segment, the script calls for me to sing *He*, a song that reminds us of God's total forgiveness. In addition to singing, I also use sign language for the deaf, to enhance the presentation.

Before the show I had to do a run-through of this song for a sound check. But as soon as I heard the first notes of the intro, tears welled up in my eyes. I tried to sing, but my voice kept breaking. I couldn't remember the signs for the words. Now this song is brief and beautiful, but on that day, although it seemed even more beautiful, it also seemed very long. I just couldn't do it.

Then I heard myself say, "Okay, Nick, you're going to have to help me on this one." As soon as those words were out of my mouth, I heard two chimes loud and clear. I looked behind me and saw a wall clock. I thought to myself, "Oh, great! With everything else I have to deal with, now I'm going to have a clock going off during my act!"

I asked the woman who was setting the tables if this clock was going to chime every hour.

She said, "What clock?"

"This one," I said, pointing to the wall behind me.

She called to a guy working in the bar area. "Hey, Dick, did you ring the toast chime?"

The reply came, "Nope, I'm nowhere near it."

It was then that I learned that this wasn't a clock at all. It was actually an "Elks Lodge Eleventh Hour Toast Chime." These chimes can be found in virtually every Elks hall in the country. Every night, at 11 o'clock, Elks offer a toast to those members who have passed on.

41 SIGNS of HOPE

They ring the chime and have a drink. It was a chime that could be sounded only by pushing a button. But nobody pushed the button that morning.

It was Nick, sending me the very first of many signs to come.

-4-
Last Words

To so many of the stories in this book, I guess you could just say, "Oh wow, that's really interesting. But there must be some explanation!" And I wouldn't blame you. Believe me, I've said that to myself over and over again. But I know now that there are just some things that have no "logical" explanation.

Shortly after Nick passed, his brother Chris gave their mom, Joanne, a book he found while cruising a local Borders Books & Music store. The book was Robert Brown's *We Are Eternal*. Robert Brown, who wrote the foreword to this book, is a well known spiritual medium from England. His book is a combination autobiography and insight into the world of spirit communication.

Reading *We Are Eternal* gave Joanne a kind of hope she had never expected to get from a book. As the expression goes, she "couldn't put it down," although putting it down one night resulted in her having a very uplifting experience the next morning.

After closing the book one evening, Joanne placed it on the floor next to our bed, then placed her glasses on top. Although she felt the book offered great comfort and encouragement, a book cannot stop the sorrow of losing a child. That night, as with so many nights before, she cried herself to sleep.

The next morning Joanne was just waking up and getting her bearings. As she swung her legs over the side of the bed, she looked down to make sure she didn't step on her glasses. That's when she saw it. Sitting on top of the book was a white feather … a pristine, beautiful white feather. Before you say it, we don't have a feather comforter or goose-down pillows.

It was this happening, along with the book, that motivated Joanne to write to Robert Brown. It wasn't an easy letter to write. Joanne told him that his book had changed her life. For the first time since the fire, she felt hope. She began to understand that death is not an end as much as a new beginning. Although Joanne doesn't remember everything she said in her letter, she does remember telling Robert about Nick and asking for a private reading.

During that time I was still answering Joanne's cellular telephone for her, as she didn't feel comfortable taking calls just yet. One night, while we were visiting Joanne's sister Julie, the cell phone rang. I asked who was calling, and the voice said, "My name is Pam Pasieka. I'm Robert Brown's personal assistant."

You can imagine how excited Joanne was to get this call. Pam said she'd read Joanne's letter and was very touched. But she wouldn't show the letter to her boss. Instead, Pam arranged for us to be Robert's very first appointment when he went to New York City in September.

The time between that call and our trip to New York was not uneventful. In early September I had a heart attack. Actually I had two heart attacks, resulting in emergency bypass surgery.

Roughly three weeks after my surgery, we took the train to the Big Apple. After arriving at Penn Station, we hailed a taxi and got to Robert's apartment two hours early. We spent the time in a coffee shop across the street, talking about our expectations. Joanne and I were both very hopeful.

We entered the Park Avenue building, and Joanne did as she was instructed. She asked for Robert Brown and gave only her first name to the doorman. I'm sure this doorman knew who Robert Brown was, and he certainly must have had an idea what our visit was about. But it was still an odd feeling to see him smile as he used the house phone to announce us.

Old buildings have old elevators, and this place was no exception. The ride in this cramped cage with the aged dials and buttons just added to the intrigue and our anticipation. As we got off the elevator we were greeted by a short, stocky man with a very gentle demeanor.

It took me a few seconds to realize that this was Robert Brown. I don't know what I was expecting, but this wasn't it.

Robert introduced himself, then led us into his apartment and offered us a seat on his couch. He didn't waste time. First he told us that he taped all sessions for his clients because he found that much of what he says may not make sense until the recorded session is heard. His next statement was what I would call a "disclaimer": a brief instruction about expectations. He told us that we might not hear from the person we were hoping to, that we should clear our minds and try to be open to whomever came through.

Then Robert began the reading. His first statement was, "Now there is a young man standing between you. He says that he is the reason you're here."

Then, for the next forty-five minutes, this gentle, unassuming man told us not just what we were hoping to hear but something we never expected to hear. The session was unbelievable. Robert gave details and names. He talked about family members, living and passed.

Our appointment time was coming to an end, and our heads were reeling from this experience! We couldn't believe the accuracy of what he had told us to that point.

Then we heard Robert say, "He wants me to tell you one more thing. He wants me to say, 'The show must go on!'"

We were utterly dumbfounded. "The show must go on" were the last words Nick said as he left me on the day before The Station fire.

"The show must go on." This couldn't have been a guess or some psychic shot in the dark. This had to be directly from Nick. It was what he said, what he believed, and how he lived his brief but abundant life.

Nick, the show *will* go on, my son, and it will always be dedicated to you!

-5-
Nick's Call

In the days that followed the fire, I found myself doing what I do best, looking after others. This isn't because I'm some kind of superhero. Quite the contrary. It's just how I have always dealt with tragedy in my life.

When my mother died, I was the one who made the arrangements. I wanted everything to go smoothly. I wanted everyone to be okay. I tried to make sure that her siblings, all elderly, were looked after and supported. Looking back on it I'm sure that everyone at the time thought I was in shock. Maybe I was, but doing these things helped fend off my own grief and kept it from "doing me in" completely.

The Station nightclub fire took place on a Thursday night. But for days afterward we heard nothing about the remains of our beloved Nick. I don't know if I can even describe what that's like. The logical side of you knows that soon the call will come. But there is another side, the side that dares to think, dares to imagine, dares to pray and, yes, even silently begs that there is some kind of mistake. That side grips tightly to one last "what if?" But, as the days wear on, that grip slowly loosens, and the hope slips from your heart.

As the news of Nicky's passing spread, our phones began to ring. They never stopped, and I always answered: the house phone, Joanne's cell and my own. I was taking calls from family, friends, work associates and the media. Everyone wanted to know the details of this horrible event and how they could help. Soon every call seemed to be just like every other: the same questions, the same answers.

Then on Monday, four days after the fire, Joanne's phone rang. When I looked at the call screen, it said, "Nicky." My heart raced. My thoughts ran wild! I immediately envisioned Nick roaming the streets, totally unaware of what had happened. I let myself entertain the dream that he had somehow escaped unharmed. All these thoughts occurred in a nanosecond. As I answered the phone, I heard myself scream, "Hello!"

There was no one at the other end.

At that moment I was filled with panic. Was it Nick? Was he trying to reach us? Did someone steal his phone? Was someone playing a very unfunny joke? I had to know!

I called AT&T and spoke with a supervisor. After I explained the situation, she had the call traced. She said the phone had been turned on around 12:50 that afternoon. It was turned on again just before I got the call, around 3:45 p.m. I tried to make sense of this. I thought that perhaps the rescue team must have found Nick, and they were examining his cell phone in an attempt to determine who he was. I was sure that while they were going through his directory looking for clues, they called Joanne's phone by mistake. I was also sure that we would hear from the authorities before the night was over.

We did. The next day I went to the funeral parlor to get the only article found with Nick, his cell phone. It was unmarred; not a scratch. I decided to keep it and use it as a special way to keep part of him with me every day. As I took the phone out of the plastic bag, I couldn't believe its good condition. It made me feel better somehow.

I turned the phone on and dialed a number, but nothing happened. I tried again…still nothing. I turned the phone off and turned it back on, but I couldn't get that phone to do a thing. We were told that the phone had been damaged by the water from the fire hoses.

Then I understood. It couldn't have been some rescue worker's fumbling that rang Joanne's phone that day. It was Nick, letting us know that our torturous, four-day vigil was over.

-6-
Wipers

You may have heard that the presence of spirits is often signaled by what appears to be an electrical malfunction. Sometimes lights flicker or an appliance will start by itself. Most of the time these instances are written off as a short circuit or faulty wiring. There's always a "logical explanation," or is there?

One day the windshield wipers on my car turned on all by themselves. At first I didn't think much of it. After all, problems with automobile electrical systems are common. It wasn't until I realized how often this was happening that I began to take notice. While driving along, my wipers would suddenly start. Of course, it would happen when I was thinking about Nick. After all, there is seldom a time when I'm not thinking about Nick.

Then I noticed that this was happening at 41 minutes past the hour. At 2:41 or 5:41. It was very odd.

I host a radio talk show, and I need to stay informed about the day's news. While in the car I always listen to AM talk radio. But one morning, while headed for the radio station where I work, I found myself listening to FM. This was very unusual for me. I was just about to pull into a gas station when my wipers started going crazy. They were going back and forth like I had turned the wiper knob to top speed. But I hadn't touched it. While watching them whipping across my windshield, I was suddenly aware of the song that was playing on the radio. The song was Norman Greenbalm's *Spirit in the Sky*. The song is about a belief that there is indeed a "spirit in the sky."

When I realized what song was playing, it brought the biggest smile to my face and a few tears as well. Now, for most people that would be enough, but not for Nick. You see, a few days later I was in Boston with Nick's brother David. I was telling him about the latest musical message I'd had from Nick.

As I finished telling the story, David smiled, then reached over and punched a button on my radio. At that very moment, we heard the disc jockey say, "And now, by special request, here is Norman Greenbalm's *Spirit in the Sky*." You can imagine how shocked we were. Oh, not because they were playing that song, but because as soon as the first notes hit the air, my car's windshield wipers began flying left and right.

-7-
Disney Dent

In 2004 Nick's brother Chris and his fiancée, Leah, were preparing for their wedding. They were doing pretty well, too. All the details were coming together nicely. The minister was hired, and they were going to exchange vows on a beach. The wedding party was selected, and everything was going beautifully.

The happy couple had even made all the plans for their honeymoon. Nothing else would do but a Disney Cruise. Yep, for these kids it was "The Mouse" all the way. The only thing missing for that dream to come true was the money. Like most young couples, there was a bit of a gap between their dreams and their pocket book. It looked for awhile like they'd have to change their plans.

But just for awhile.

On my way to a doctor's appointment one day, I stopped at a traffic light. A car hit me from behind. When I got out, I realized that the car had been pushed into me by a city public-works truck. The back door on my van was buckled, and there were a few other minor dings, but no one was hurt. So it was no big deal. After giving the police my information, I continued to my appointment.

Later that afternoon I spoke with someone at the city solicitor's office. I was told to get three estimates, and that they would take care of the damage. Over the next few days I dutifully collected my estimates, delivered them to City Hall, and forgot about it.

About two weeks later, Joanne got a call from Chris. He told her that he and Leah's plan to save all the money they needed for their honeymoon was not working out. Weddings are expensive, and they just didn't think they could do it. Chris asked Joanne if we could help them.

When Joanne hung up, she said, "The kids need $1,500 to go on their honeymoon."

"That's nothing. I only need three and a half inches to be six feet tall," I quipped. "I think we're both going to be disappointed."

Of course I was just kidding, but we really couldn't think of how to help Chris and Leah. Joanne and I began wracking our brains, then it hit me.

"Hey," I said. "I'm going to get that check from the car accident. I really don't need to fix my car right now. Let's give the money to the kids."

Joanne thought it was a super idea, and we were so relieved. As any parent knows, helping your kids is Job One.

Now, I'd love to take credit for this idea. This kind of boost is just what my ego needs. But, as I would soon find out, the idea wasn't mine. As I already mentioned, I went out and collected the estimates requested by the city. I saw them all. I knew roughly what I would receive for the reimbursement for my damage. One estimate was for $1,728. The other was for $1,678, and the third was for $1,400 even.

So you can imagine my surprise when the check I received from the city was for none of those amounts. Instead, it was a check for $1,536.41. I couldn't figure how they arrived at that number, but it ended in a "41," so it was okay with me!

The next night, Joanne and I went to a Hot Rod Car Rally at a city park. We strolled through the cars and listened to the '50s music.

During our walk, we talked about this whole incident with the accident. We talked about how the kids needed help with their honeymoon, and how the check, which ended in 41, came right on time. Joanne and I were sure that Nick had planned this whole thing. Just then, Joanne spotted a license plate on a vintage automobile. The car was shiny and new looking, even though it was a good forty years old. The license plate on the car was "OUR 41."

As we admired the car, I heard a man shout, "Hey, Dave!"

We turned around to see a guy who looked very familiar. He said,

"Gee, I'm really sorry about hitting you guys the other day, but the brakes locked up and my truck wouldn't stop."

I couldn't believe it. This was the man who was driving the city truck that caused not only a chain reaction of cars but a chain reaction of events that helped Nick send the kids on their honeymoon cruise!

-8-
Candles

Chris was the oldest boy. Nick was the youngest. But you would never have guessed they were ten years apart. You see, Nick and Chris were closer and more connected than any two siblings I've ever known. They shared a deep and abiding love for music, theater, family, fun, church and each other.

I suppose there are several ways to describe this bond. If I thought about it for a while, some tired old cliché might come to mind. But it would be inadequate. These boys were bound to each other at the heart; there was a silver cord that tethered them. Since Nick's passing, that cord has acted as a sort of spiritual clothesline filled with the clean, bright, fresh-scented memories of true brotherly love.

Let me point out here that Chris and Nick were real brothers. They had their disagreements and conflicts. They would do battle and then make up, just like other brothers. Chris was older and more "laid back." He's a gentle, respectful, pleasant young man. Nick, on the other hand, could be a real imp when inclined. He loved to "bust," and he had a unique way of irritating you while making you laugh until you cried.

One night shortly before the fire, Chris was trying to get some sleep. So, of course, Nick decided to start a sing-a-long. Positioning himself next to Chris's bed, Nick loudly strummed his guitar while singing old show tunes. Of course, Nick had changed the words to these songs, inserting instead, shall we say, some rather indelicate lyrics about people he and Chris knew. At this point Chris had two battles going on. One was trying to get to sleep. The other was trying not to laugh. He knew that if he gave in to the latter, that would be all the encouragement Nick needed.

The odd thing about that night was something Nick said. In an effort to enlist Chris's help in this song fest, Nick chimed: "Okay, Chris, let's all sing the songs from that great old musical, *Carousel*." A short time later, Nick said, "I don't know why I said that. I don't even know what *Carousel* is about!"

What Nick didn't know, at least on a conscious level, is that *Carousel* is about the passing of a young boy who returns to watch over his family.

From the time Nick was very young, he and Chris shared a special tradition. Chris's birthday is in June. And every year, as people stood around the table waiting to sing *Happy Birthday*, Chris would let Nick blow out his candles. This was something they both looked forward to. It became a running joke. "Happy birthday, Chris! Okay, Nicky, blow out the candles." Of course, this was one tradition that stopped when Nick passed. Or did it?

In June 2003 we were planning Chris's birthday celebration. This was a difficult time for everyone. What should have been a happy occasion was clouded by the absence of Chris's designated "candle putter outer."

For his birthday that year, Chris had asked for a video camera. We had put his present in a gift bag and planned to give it to him during our ride to the restaurant for his birthday dinner. We had several people in the van: Chris, his fiancé, Leah; Gabby (Nick's girlfriend); Alex (Gabby's brother) and Joanne. I was driving.

Joanne handed the gift bag to Chris. He reached in and took out his present. Of course he was very pleased. But as he started to open the box, he stopped for a moment and said, "I guess I'm going to have to blow out my own candles this year." It got very quiet.

Chris pulled the box open and took out a brochure that was folded on the top. It was then that I heard Gabby gasp, "Oh, isn't that cute!"

Then I heard Chris say "Oh, my God. Mom, look, look!"

On the front of that brochure was a picture of a five-year-old boy blowing out the candles on a birthday cake! At first we were shocked, then we were completely stunned. The young boy whose picture

The boy on the brochure, left, and Nicky at age 7.

was on the front of this Samsung video brochure, the five-year-old who was blowing out the candles on a birthday cake, was identical to Nick when he was five. The resemblance was so remarkable that Gabby thought Joanne and I had put Nick's picture in the box.

Gabby believes this was Nick's way of keeping a tradition, and so do we... Happy Birthday, Chris!

Author's Note

I used Microsoft Word ® to type this story into my computer. When I wrote that Nick was twelve years younger than Chris, the spell checker underlined the words "twelve years," indicating an error. I checked to see if I had misspelled twelve. I hadn't. Then I checked to see if I had improperly spaced the words. I didn't. I tried putting commas in and taking commas out, all to no avail. The error line stayed.

When I finished the story, I called Joanne in to read it to her. When I read the line that said the boys were twelve years apart, Joanne said, "Ten years." I changed the twelve to ten, and the line disappeared! I guess this book is going to have more than one editor. *DK*

-9-
They Walk Among Us

Our friend psychic medium Cindy Gilman told Joanne and me about something Nick had written that was very special, something different from all his other writings. We looked through his room again, but we didn't find anything. Then, about two weeks later, Nick's friend Emily called Chris to tell him that she had found the script of a play Nick had written.

After reading *They Walk Among Us*, we realized just how special it was.

When he was sixteen, Nick was a member of the All Children's Theater (ACT) in Pawtucket, Rhode Island. ACT was a theater group for children up to age eighteen. One of the friends Nick made at ACT was Sam Adrain. Sam was younger than Nick, only nine years old. But Nick loved kids, and Sam really looked up to Nick.

During Nick's last year with this group, ACT announced its annual play-writing competition. Members were encouraged to write an original, one-act play, and the winner would have his or her entry performed on stage. I remember Nick mentioning something about writing a play, but he never talked much about it, and it wasn't until Emily found the script, after Nick passed, that we learned the story of *They Walk Among Us*.

It's an inspiring story about young people who die and return as guardian angels. The play features three teen angels: two boys, Levi and Cyrus, and a charming girl angel named Grace. We don't know why Nick chose those names. I was surprised that he didn't at least name the girl angel Gabby, after the love of his life. But as with everything else about Nick and his brief life, there was always a reason.

They Walk Among Us is a warm, funny and uplifting story about hope, belief, caring, spirituality and, of course, love. The three main characters, although different in many ways, share a mission and a common goal. The mission is to help their "assignments" work their way through troubled times, and their goal is to reassure them of God's unconditional love.

It was just after the ACT play competition had been announced that Sam Adrain's sister, a beautiful little girl with blond hair and a radiant smile, took seriously ill. She was rushed to the hospital and passed away in a matter of hours. This precious five-year-old had passed of the same rare virus that took the life of Muppet creator Jim Henson. Now I think I know why Nick chose at least one of the names he did. Sam's little sister's name is Grace.

After he finished the first draft, Nick e-mailed the play to his brother Chris to edit and critique. They chatted about it a few times, but Nick never submitted it to the competition. I don't know why. Maybe he felt it was too long or too spiritual or too something. Whatever it was, *They Walk Among Us* never made it to the stage before Nick's passing.

Instead this stirring play, with all its humor, encouragement and compassion, was relegated to a stack of Nick's other "works in progress."

I believe that many events surrounding the eventual production of this play, the time it was written, the name of the girl angel and, of course, the subject matter, all come together to give real witness that *They Walk Among Us* is more than just a title.

The play had to be produced. We just couldn't let this script sit on a shelf. Of course only one person would be able to do justice to Nick's play: his brother Chris. Chris is ten years older than Nick, but the age difference never seemed to matter. They were always so much more than brothers.

Chris knew Nick, really knew him. And he really loved and supported Nick. So the task was Chris's. It was his job to see that *They Walk Among Us* came to life, Nick's love note to the world.

The first of what would be three incarnations of Nick's master-piece was produced at a church in Pawtucket. It was rather rough and hastily put together. The cast, all Nick's friends, performed on the altar, in the pulpit and up the aisles of the church. The audience sat in the pews. There was little time for rehearsal or blocking, never mind learning lines, so the play was presented in a format called "staged reading." This meant that the actors actually carried scripts with them during the show.

In addition to *They Walk Among Us* that night, Nick's girlfriend, Gabby, and her parents, Chuck and Consuelo Sherba, offered a brief concert after the play. The Sherbas are very talented and profes-sional musicians, and they brought some friends who played and sang, then did dramatic readings. It was a great night, and it ended perfectly.

Chris hadn't timed the play, and he didn't know how long Gabby's, parents had planned to perform. So you can appreciate how we felt when we realized that the play and the concert had ended at exactly 9:41!

And the saga continued.

Shortly after The Station fire, we were invited back to ACT for a fundraiser for Nick's scholarship fund. In attendance that night was Jon Land, a Rhode Island native and an internationally published au-thor of thrillers. Jon came to the event that night just to meet Joanne and me. He had read an article about Nick by Channing Gray, a the-ater critic for the *Providence Journal*. After reading the article, Jon had felt an odd affinity for Nick. Even though they had never met, this article and the impact it had on Jon made him want to know more about our son. Jon contacted Wren Goodrum, founder of ACT, and told her he wanted to meet Nick's parents. Wren told Jon he could meet us at the fundraiser, and there we all were.

Wren introduced us to Jon, and I liked him from the start. He was affable and open, and he has a sincerity that makes people around him feel comfortable and relaxed. After speaking briefly that night, we made plans to have lunch later in the week. That lunch marked the beginning of what has become a very close friendship. Jon had literally hundreds of questions, and we were glad to answer. It was great talking about Nick, especially with someone so interested in knowing all about him. Chris came along for the meeting, too. It turned out that he and Jon shared many interests.

Chris told Jon about *They Walk Among Us*, and Jon said he was anxious to read the play, so Chris got a copy to him. After reading it, Jon couldn't wait to call us. Almost immediately he had several ideas for this beautiful, poignant work. Jon told us that he wanted to turn Nick's play into a feature-length motion picture. There was no doubt in Jon's mind that there was much more to this story of three teen angels.

If this was going to happen, there was a lot to do, and it all started with one very important sign. Jon wouldn't even consider doing this project without giving Nick the full credit as author. To properly market the script, Jon would have to enroll Nick as a member of the Writers Guild of America. Jon took care of everything. He filled out the paperwork, paid the enrollment fee, then had the "Document of Registration" sent to our home.

I'm sure you can imagine our excitement when we opened the envelope. But I don't think you can guess what we found. The official certificate from the Writer's Guild of America read:

Intellectual Property Registry
Material entitled: *They Walk Among Us*
By Jon Land – Writer
Nick O'Neill – Writer
Material Type: Screenplay
The registration number was 9409<u>41</u>

Yes, Nick's first membership card as a professional writer carried his special number, 41. But that was only the beginning. As it turned out, *They Walk Among Us*, the movie, would mark Jon's 41st project.

Jon would say later that it was his first successful collaboration. You'll see just how much of a collaboration it was.

-10-
Kunkel's 41

He called her Kunkel. Oh, she had a first name: Emily. But Nick just called her Kunkel.

About a year after Nick's passing, Kunkel was working on the East Side of Providence in a store called OOP! It was one of those trendy, jigs and jocks kind of stores where you could buy anything from calendars to candlesticks. Emily had to close that night and wasn't feeling especially high. She had just been notified that she had been deferred from Fordham University, and she was beginning to worry a bit about her future.

Shortly before closing time, a man came into the store who bore a strong resemblance to Nick. He even wore a suede jacket and had a haircut just like her old friend's. Kunkel watched the man browse for awhile, but couldn't hold herself back. As Kunkel approached the man she was suddenly engulfed in a scent she recognized immediately. It was the aroma of the house where Nick and his family had lived. It was more than just a smell. It brought Kunkel back to some of the happiest times of her young life, the days at 88 Wentworth Avenue.

Kunkel suddenly realized that she had been doing two things, reminiscing about her days with Nick, and staring at the customer. She woke from her reverie when her Nick look-a-like, or "Nickalike," as she called him, asked to see some salt and pepper shakers. Kunkel showed him what she had, and he made his choice.

As she rang up the sale, the total came to $40.61. This made her smile because 61 is Kunkel's lucky number. But, as she told us later, Nick had a more obvious "hello" in store. You see, the man in the suede jacket with a haircut just like Nick's fished around in his pockets, looking for the 61 cents. Then he stopped, handed Kunkel two twenties and a one with the words, "Here, take 41."

41 SIGNS of HOPE

-11-
Keeping Time
to the Music

Among his many talents, Nick was a prolific composer. By the time he was eighteen he had written over fifty songs. Eight of those songs were featured on *Day Has Turned to Evening,* the CD he recorded with his band, Shryne.

After Nick passed we wanted to do something special with his music. We wanted to find a way to use his beautiful songs to do some good for others. So the Nicky O' Foundation, a charity for aspiring young musicians, was born. This organization would fund music lessons and instrument rentals for young people who otherwise couldn't afford them. We planned to use the money from Nick's CD sales to fund this project. But the CD had already been released, and we weren't sure how much interest there would be in a second release.

It was around this time that we found a cassette tape in Nick's room. It was a recording of Nick playing his guitar and singing all alone. He was singing a song he had just written about his girlfriend, Gabby. It was called *My Little Girl*. That's when we decided to add *My Little Girl* as a bonus cut and re-release his CD. We used the whole recording, unedited, with guitar tuning and all. We didn't want to mar the purity of this find. Now, I didn't pay any attention to the length of the song. After all, even with nine cuts, there would still be plenty of room for it on the CD.

So *Day Has Turned to Evening* was re-released with *My Little Girl*. But it wasn't until almost a year after its release that one of Nicky's friends told us that Nick's solo tribute to Gabby ran five minutes and 41 seconds.

-12-
Palm Sunday

I've always been impressed with the spirituality of Nick's brothers, Chris, Billy and David. From the time they were very young they enjoyed going to church. They were always part of the pageants at Christmas and Easter, weekend retreats, and even the church-sponsored "haunted house" at Halloween. They loved being part of their church community.

Chris especially enjoyed Palm Sunday. This is the time when Christians offer palm branches to one another as a symbol of peace. Chris often would make small crosses with the palm branches. He never missed a Palm Sunday Mass.

The year Nick passed, Chris was hired to direct *Lend me a Tenor*, for a community theater group in Saugus, Massachusetts. The play was to be presented in a local church hall. The last show for *Tenor* fell on Palm Sunday, and this meant that Chris would have to miss his first Palm Sunday Mass ever.

That night, after striking the set and attending the cast party, Chris and his wife, Leah, headed for home. While driving, Chris kept thinking about missing Palm Sunday. Then he started to think about how many things had changed since Nick passed, and he couldn't help but wonder how many more changes were to come. Just then, Chris realized that he had left his jacket back at the church.

He turned the car around and returned to the now-empty building.

As he entered, the hall was dark. The echo of his footsteps could be heard through the building. Chris walked backstage, and he could see that his jacket had been tossed on the floor in a corner of the room. As he got closer, there appeared to be something on his jacket. Chris bent down and, as his eyes adjusted to the light, he could see that on his jacket lay two palm branches.

-13-
Magic Kingdom

Nick loved anything Disney. He especially loved Walt Disney World, and our family made a pilgrimage almost every year to this wonderful Florida resort. Near the end of the year Nick passed, we made another visit. The mood was a strange combination of elation and sadness. We started every day with a childlike excitement dampened with a longing sadness. There was a desire to see Nick's smiling face and childlike exuberance once again.

Of course a trip to Disney promised many reminders from Nick that he was right there with us. When we arrived at Orlando International Airport, our car was late. We had to wait a bit for our white stretch limo to arrive. This delay put us on the right track because it caused our car to arrive at Disney World at exactly 7:41.

We had a great sleep that first night. But on the second morning at Disney, Joanne and I were awakened by a bedside alarm clock that no one had set. It woke us at 4:41 a.m.

One of Nick's favorite features at Disney World was the Hoop-Dee-Doo Revue. This is an old-time country music dinner show set in a western saloon. They serve buckets of chicken, ribs, potatoes and soft drinks. The show is a collection of down-home humor, songs and skits. It's very much a family show, and our whole crew attended that evening.

Hoop-Dee-Doo Revue takes place at Fort Wilderness, on the op-

**PIONEER HALL
HOOP-DEE-DOO MUSICAL REVUE**

41

DATE   TABLE NO.

9

NO. IN PARTY

O'Neill

NAME

When seating begins, please return to the entrance,
And we will escort you to your table.
Please remember that tables are pre-assigned.
GRATUITY INCLUDED IN TICKET PRICE

A ticket to Disney's Hoop-Dee-Doo Revue assigns the family to table 41.

posite side of the lake from the Magic Kingdom. We decided to take the ferry across the lake. As we arrived at the dock, Joanne suddenly said, "Here we go Nick, Hoop-Dee-Doo Revue!" Just as she said it, *all* the lights on the dock blinked off and on! Then Joanne went to the window to pick up our tickets. This took her a few minutes because of the crowd. When she returned she was smiling but also looked a little dazed. She came up to me with a card.

"Look at the table number we've been assigned…table number 41!"

At that moment a blonde-haired boy not more than five years old ran past us. And we heard a woman I presume was his mother call out, "Nicholas, come back here!"

-14-
David's 41

For Christmas 2005 Nick's brother David asked for a flip phone and a new phone number. You see, David has moved to New York to pursue an acting career. So he needed a number within the local area code. This was no easy task. First we couldn't get him a new phone without shutting off the one he had. We had to wait until just the right moment. God forbid he should be without a phone for a day. Well, we finally worked out that part of it.

Now all we had to do was get the new number. This turned out to be another pain. Joanne called AT&T to get the change started. She gave the operator all the information, and she waited while they confirmed the details. Then they told Joanne that it would take another half hour or so, and that they would call her back. Half an hour later, Joanne answered the phone and the lady on the other end said, "Do you have a pencil? Here's your new number." It ended in 93<u>41</u>."

"Merry Christmas, David!" Love, Nick.

-15-
Photo Play

"I'm ready for my close-up, Mr. DeMille."

I think my family has more photos, movies and videotaped memories than most any other. You could actually use these snapshots and footage as "time lapse" photography. You can literally watch our boys morph into handsome young men.

Chris, Nick's oldest brother, is the archivist. He keeps the records. There are stacks of photo albums, videotapes and neatly kept correspondence. If you're looking for any remembrance of the past, just ask Chris. He not only knows where to find it, but he can give you "chapter and verse" on what happened, who was there, and what was said.

Just two years after the fire, Joanne wanted to copy portions of some of the tapes. Her idea was to build a collection of some of Nick's funniest performances. There was a Christmas cabaret with his pal Matt, the impromptu Easter Sunday ballad about some "colorful" relatives and, of course, his hilarious *haiku* at his brother Billy's wedding.

Accomplishing this task called for jury-rigging a dubbing setup using two VCRs and a handful of wires. There was certainly an easier way to do this. After all, I work with broadcast professionals every day. But Joanne loved watching these clips over and over again. As we all sat around watching, Joanne suddenly said that she could feel

Nick watching with us. Now this wasn't unusual for Joanne; she felt Nick all the time. The tape of Billy's wedding was playing. Suddenly the tape briefly froze. Then, with the word "Play" still displayed on the screen, the tape began to re-wind.

We couldn't figure out what was happening. We looked around to see if someone was playing with the remote or maybe accidentally sitting on it. But no. The tape machine had changed modes all on its own. It was rewinding while still displaying the word "Play."

Then it froze again, this time on a closeup of Nick's smiling face. You can imagine our joy and feelings of warmth when this happened! I told you that what Joanne felt wasn't unusual for her. Neither were the actions of the "phantom tape player."

You see, it was just typical Nick.

-16-
Take Your Seat

I've worked as a talk radio host for more than thirty-five years, and the job can be more than a little challenging. It's no small task to come up with fresh ideas and new topics every day. But every once in a while an idea will come from "out of the blue."

I had one of those inspirations while we were preparing to do *They Walk Among Us* for the second anniversary of the fire. I was driving into work one morning, thinking about how quickly our lives changed when Nick passed. I was thinking about how none of us knows when it will be our time to pass. In scripture, it says, "Watch therefore, for ye know neither the day nor the hour...." (Matthew 25:13)

I realized that I could actually talk to someone on my show that day, and that they might pass right after hanging up. That gave me a great idea. I decided to pose a question to my audience.

"Okay," I said, "You have just two hours to live. What are you going to do with the time?"

I gave my listeners the assignment of deciding what they would do with the last two hours of their lives.

Well, I can tell you that my phones did not ring off the hook. I really had to "walk them through it." Not only had people not thought much about this, they were not especially interested in being made to think or talk about it. At first, I got a few calls with just the kind of responses you might expect.

"Dave, I would gather my family and tell them how much I love them."

"You know, Dave, I think I would go and sit by the ocean."

Oh, and there was: "Dave, if I had just two hours to live, I would go out and run up every credit card I had to buy gifts for all my loved ones. What the heck? I'm not even going have to make the first payment!"

Then a young man named Mike called, told me that if he only had the two hours I allotted him he would make a phone call. It seems that Mike had an old friend he hadn't seen for many years. He told me that they had always been very close, but somehow had lost touch over the years. I was surprised at this call. I mean it seemed so simple. What's the big deal? Just pick up the phone. Call the guy! Which is exactly what I told Mike, and I really tried to push him to take action.

About a week later, Mike called back and told me that he had chased down his old friend. They spoke on the phone for a long time and had even met for coffee. Then Mike told me that he and his recycled buddy were coming to see *They Walk Among Us*, which was to be shown locally at the Stadium Theatre in Woonsocket, Rhode Island.

It's important at this point that I mention two interesting facts.

The first is that the main plot line of *They Walk Among Us* deals with a young man in a personal conflict over being homosexual. The angels assure the character, Adam Tyler, that there is no need to feel lost or alone. They tell him that he is a child of God and is loved now and always, unconditionally.

The second is that Mike himself is homosexual. I realized how cool Nick would think it was that these lifelong pals, one gay, one straight, would share seeing his play. And indeed Nick *did* think it was cool. How do I know? Because when Mike and his friend came to the theater that night, they bought their tickets and proceeded to their seats. Mike's ticket was for the fourth row, second seat, and his old friend's ticket was for the fourth row, first seat.

This seat in the Stadium Theatre bears the plaque that reads, "In loving memory of Nick O'Neill, Encore Performer."

-17-
Night of Angels

This show at the Stadium Theatre was the second performance of *They Walk Among Us.* Chris wanted to give his brother's sensitive and beautiful creation the kind of presentation it deserved. He wanted this night to be a moving and powerful celebration of Nick and his work, and Chris knew just how to do it.

In addition to ACT, Nick also had belonged to the Encore Repertory Company, a community theater group affiliated with the Stadium Theatre. After Nick passed, Encore and the Stadium started a scholarship in Nick's name. The grants would go to college students majoring in theater. Nick had appeared in many Encore productions. As always, he brought all he could to each performance. He acted, sang, danced, clowned and enthralled audiences through every show.

Nick played Conrad Birdie in *Bye, Bye, Birdie.* He was the Scarecrow in *The Wizard of Oz.* He had multiple parts in the Broadway reviews, and he hosted Encore's highly successful Christmas Cabaret with his buddy, Matt DeThomas. This cabaret featured seasonal music and lots of comedy. Nick and Matt were a great duo. Their style was reminiscent of the great comedy teams Abbott and Costello, Martin and Lewis, and the Smothers Brothers. Nick loved to make people laugh, and they loved it when he did.

It was because of this connection to Encore and the Stadium that Chris decided to offer something more that night. It would be a special evening. Using Encore cast members, along with over thirty of Nick's family members and friends, the night became a loving remembrance of Nick and his talent.

The evening would be called "A Night of Angels."

The first half of the show was a musical salute. One by one, the performers took center stage in front a big screen that showed pictures of Nick. Matt DeThomas did most of the songs that Nick had performed during his time with Encore. The other players did other songs that featured Nick over the years, along with songs that carried a special message.

Nick's brother Bill sang *You Lift Me Up*, which honors and gives thanks for the support and inspiration of a loved one. Bill's voice is resounding and rich, and his ability to interpret a song is a wonderful gift that we have all enjoyed for many years. The love and sentiment he displayed that night, the beautiful, melodious sound of his voice, and the words he sang touched us all.

The second half of the show was the first full-stage production of *They Walk Among Us*. When I say full-stage production, I mean sets, props, music, backdrops, costumes, makeup, sound, and the beautiful Stadium stage. We were ready. You could feel the love in the theater that night. It was like the entire audience was locked in a huge spiritual embrace.

The play began with the entrance of the three angels: Levi, played by Gabby's brother, Alex; Grace, played by Nick's girlfriend, Gabby; and Cyrus, the part Nick had written for himself, played masterfully by Nick's brother David. From the opening music to the final exit of the angels, the audience was spellbound. At the end, the cast stood to what was much more than a standing ovation. It was a genuine outpouring of love and appreciation.

It's sometimes hard for me to imagine that a boy of just sixteen could write such funny, enlightening and moving dialogue. The message of *They Walk Among Us* is one that most people would consider too deep and spiritually evolved for someone so young. Nick's story of hope, faith and unconditional love is one that those in the attendance won't soon forget. The wonderful way the performers, cast and crew celebrated Nick that night, and the impact of Nick's touching story of acceptance and forgiveness, truly made February 20, 2004, "A Night of Angels."

-18-
On the Tube

We were elated with the success of "Night of Angels." During the summer of 2004, Joanne and I reminisced about what a great show it was. I remember Joanne saying that she would love to be able to do it every year. But she knew that would be next to impossible. After all, that would mean trying to get the same cast and crew together. Many of them had gone off to college. David had moved to New York, and other cast members had scattered hither and yon. Then there were props, scenery, costumes, the list goes on and on.

"We couldn't possibly do it every year," I said. "But we could do it one more time and tape it!"

That way we could do it once and show it on television every year. What a novel idea for someone who works in radio and television production, huh?

We wanted to be able to finish this project by February 20, 2005, the second anniversary of the fire. This gave us almost seven months to put everything together. I wasn't sure that was long enough. But if we were going to finish this by the anniversary, it would have to be. So we got right to work.

This time *They Walk Among Us* would be performed as a stage play but produced for television.

Then we got the idea that we could do even more with this project. We could use the airing of this play as a fundraiser. The Station

Family Fund was an organization founded by Vicky Potvin, who had actually survived the fire. She and a handful of friends and supporters started this fund shortly after the fire to help victims' families and survivors with their financial and emotional recovery.

This was great! Not only would we be able to offer this play every year to a much wider audience, but we could use *They Walk Among Us* as a vehicle to help others. Nick was loving this. I could just feel it!

Producing *They Walk Among Us* for television was no small task. Although I had produced many television shows and commercials in my career, this project was special. It had to be right. There was a lot of financial and emotional pressure. I began to feel like the old joke about a dog chasing a car: If he catches it, what's he going to do with it? Well, I had not only chased it, I caught it, and now it was my job to do something with it!

Of course, Chris would direct the show. That was the easy part. The other person we needed was a videographer. We had no production budget, but I knew from experience in producing for television that this show could be done with one camera. What we needed was a professional who could shoot, edit and post-produce, while being able to cut a few corners. Well, actually, more than a few corners. As I said, we had no budget. I knew just the guy.

Christian DeRezendes was a young man I had met during "Night of Angels." He had volunteered to videotape the show for us so we could have a remembrance. Christian brought one of his cameras and set it up in the back of the theater, much as parents would do to tape their child in a dance recital.

While the crowd hunted for their seats, Christian and I chatted, and I had a good feeling about him from the beginning. He told me about a documentary he had done on the life and gifts of a psychic from out of state. He even told me about having some "feelings of his own on occasion." I knew right then that I had found the "man behind the camera."

Christian DeRezendes turned out to be much more than that. He came to be a close family friend. He is another person touched by his own connection to the number 41. Stay tuned.

-19-
The Backdrop

We had lots to do if we were going to put *They Walk Among Us* together for videotaping by the second anniversary of The Station fire. Chris was going to direct once again and, of course, he wanted everything to be just right.

To begin with, Chris wanted to order a new backdrop for the New York street scene. A backdrop is a massive canvas painting hung on the back wall of the stage to "set the scene" for shows. Depending on your choice, a backdrop can be used to depict a street scene, a library, a courtroom or any other location. If you choose correctly, these backdrops can be very realistic. Chris's choice was realistic and expensive.

I hated to sound like a typical producer, but I had to ask Chris why he just couldn't use the same backdrop we used during the previous stage performance at the Stadium Theatre. After all, it was cheaper, and our budget was practically nonexistent. But Chris had found a brand new backdrop on the Internet, one that he thought was perfect. He wanted everything just right for Nick, and he really wanted this new backdrop. I told him I would do what I could.

Because the backdrop maker wanted payment in advance, and didn't take credit cards, we had to wait until we actually had the money in hand before I could place the order. Unfortunately, that meant waiting until the last possible moment.

Chris was worried that his backdrop wouldn't arrive in time for the shoot. We had only three days to videotape the whole show, and the dates were set in stone. We were lucky enough to be able to secure the Stadium during school vacation week, which meant that cast members who had gone away to college were able to come back. Nick's brother David was able to come up from New York, and several other players arranged for time off from their jobs.

So the race was on. We ordered and paid for the backdrop, then waited. As the shoot date got closer, I began to feel the tension. I didn't even want to think about what would happen if the backdrop were late or didn't show up at all. On the day before we were to begin shooting, there was still no backdrop.

On my way to the theater, I called the company in question, and the woman I spoke with told me that it had already been shipped. Then she reminded me that I had been told when I put in my order that it would take three to five days to arrive. This didn't make me feel any better, since my order had been put in four days before.

Now all we could do was wait. I took a few minutes to say a prayer. I asked God if he could speed up the truck that was bringing our New York street scene. Then I added a little whisper to Nick, asking him if he could help us out. It seemed that I had no sooner said "Amen" when my cell phone rang. The call was from the office at the Stadium Theatre, telling me that the backdrop had been delivered to the lobby!

Thrilled and relieved, I got to the theater and found the crew hard at work. There was still so much to do! I found Chris standing near the edge of the stage, and asked if he'd seen the backdrop.

"You mean it's here?"

Obviously, no one had told him. He bolted up the aisle and, in less than a minute, came trotting back with a huge box. He was smiling almost triumphantly. As he got closer to the stage, he yelled something like "Hey, wait 'til you see this! Everybody look!" Chris came up the stairs and dropped the box on the stage.

On that box was written with black magic marker, on all four sides, the new backdrop's catalog number, a number that we found out later had not been assigned when Chris picked it out.

The number was 141.

-20-
Post Office

As I said before, you may be thinking: "Now that's interesting, but there must be a feasible explanation." And believe it or not, I would agree with you. I'm sure that if you think about it long enough you could come up with a perfectly "logical" theory about how all these things happened.

Then maybe you could help me with this one.

Christian DeRezendes entered Nick's play in the Black Point Film Festival in Lake Geneva, Wisconsin. On May 1, 2005, *They Walk Among Us* won "Best Screenplay" for a short or feature. You can imagine how excited we were. This success encouraged us to enter Nick's work in more competitions.

That same year, using a list of appropriate festivals compiled by Chris and Christian, Joanne entered *They Walk Among Us* in two additional film competitions. One was a film festival in New Hampshire, and the other was the Spiritual Film Festival in California. Because both festivals required that the entry fee be paid by money order, Joanne wrapped and addressed two copies of the movie. At the post office, she ordered a money order for each entry fee. When the clerk handed Joanne the money order for the New Hampshire entry, she did what she always does: She looked for a 41. No luck. The serial number on the receipt ended in 52.

Then the clerk gave Joanne the second money order, the one for the California event. It only makes sense that the next money order would have a sequential number. It would end in 53 or 51. Instead, the serial number on that money order, the one destined for the Spiritual Film Festival, ended with 41.

-21-
March of Dimes

Remember Nick's friend Sam Adrain from ACT, whose little sister, Grace, passed away with a deadly virus at just five years old? When Grace passed, Nick tried to take Sam, then only nine year old, under his wing in an effort to help him through his grief.

Our friend Ann Hood is Sam's and Grace's mom. We asked Ann if she would consent to be interviewed for *41 The Movie*, a video we were planning to make about Nick and many of our experiences in this book. We wanted to speak with Ann about Sam's relationship with Nick and the signs she and her husband had experienced since Grace's passing. We wanted to hear about the dimes.

You see, Grace and her dad, Lorne, shared something very special. They would go for walks to look for dimes. Hand in hand, they would stroll along, chatting about the day's events, all the while searching for lost coins. They would see pennies, nickels and even the occasional quarter, but they were only looking for dimes.

It's my guess that this excursion for loose change had nothing to do with finding money. I'm betting that this hunt for not-so-buried treasure was just an excuse for dad to steal some private time with his precious little girl. It worked, too. Grace loved their walks, and Lorne still takes them, if only in his memory.

When the time came for Ann to make her contribution to *41*, the shoot was emotional for everyone. In the movie, Ann speaks of how difficult it was to tell Sam about the fire and Nick's passing. Ann knew how much Nick's concern and kindness toward Sam had helped him make it through that impossibly tough time of Grace's passing. Now, less than a year later, it was Ann's job to tell Sam that Nick had passed as well.

After the shoot, Ann, Aidan and Sam were going out to dinner. In the car, Ann had so much to think about. She asked herself if all of this was real. She pondered the "41" signs from Nick, and the remarkable number of dimes they themselves were finding. She wondered if the dimes really were from Grace. Ann wrestled with these thoughts, trying to decide whether these were genuine signals from our loved ones or just wishful thinking. Ann wanted to believe the former, but she just wasn't sure.

When they arrived, the restaurant had just opened and was almost empty. Yet the hostess seemed to have trouble choosing a table for Ann and her family. Finally, Ann said, "It's okay. We can sit anywhere."

The hostess turned and said, "No, I have to put you at table 41." This response really caught Ann off guard. As they were being led to their table Ann couldn't get over what she had just heard. Why would the hostess say that? What would make this stranger choose table 41 of all numbers? Did someone put her up to it? Was this a joke?

I don't know if Ann got any answers to all this, but I do know that she would be asking even more questions. That's because, as the family approached table 41 and sat down, Ann looked down. There, lying on the freshly vacuumed carpet, was a shiny new dime.

-22-
41 License Plates

Our friend Jean Rondeau is executive director of the Stadium Theatre. He has been with the theater for many years, and was a key
player among those who worked so hard to bring this beautiful entertainment venue back to its original glory. This historic theater,
which first opened in 1926, had fallen on very hard times. Jean and
many other community activists raised all the money and did all the
work to see that this magnificent old theater survived.

While always a good friend, Jean was a bit of a skeptic when it
came to our "41" experiences. He didn't make a big deal out of this
reluctance to believe our stories; he just kept it to himself.

Jean was there on the night we debuted the first rendition of *41
The Movie* at the Stadium. He watched the beginning but had to leave.
Jean had just undergone surgery on his knee, and he needed to get
home and rest. When he left the theater that night, he was thinking
about what he had just seen in *41*. He wanted to get on board with all
this, but he just couldn't quite accept it.

Since Jean was on crutches and wearing a knee brace, it was quite
difficult to get to his car. When he finally made it, as Jean would tell
me later, he noticed the license plate of the car in front of his. The
plate had the number 41 on it. After watching the stories in *41*, an
odd feeling came over Jean, and he actually felt more open to the
possibilities offered in our movie.

I couldn't understand why something so incidental would bring Jean to this. For someone so skeptical to have his mind changed just by seeing one license plate with a 41 on it made me giggle.

I thought to myself, "Gee, Jean, is that all it takes?"

As we would learn, however, Jean's "sighting" was only the beginning of this story.

In our quest to understand as much as we could about the signs and messages we were getting, we met with another psychic medium from Bridgewater, Massachusetts. Maureen Hancock is an attractive woman with Irish eyes and a ready wit. We liked her immediately. At our first session with Maureen, she seemed to connect with Nick right away.

I should point out that, after Nick's passing, we made appointments with many mediums. In our search for validation and confirmation of what we were experiencing, we began a sort of quest to compare and cross-reference what we were being told. After each visit we would listen to the tape of the session and scrutinize every word. What we learned from all this was that the messages we received weren't just similar. In most cases they were virtually identical.

Maureen was a bit different in that she didn't just connect with Nick, she bonded with him. For months after our first meeting with Maureen, she would e-mail Joanne to tell her about how she was getting "41s" everywhere, and that Nick was helping her in her sessions and bringing spirits to her. She told us that when a parent who had lost a child came to see her, it was Nick who would escort the child to the session.

Yes sir, Nick and Maureen had become quite a team!

One story about this "dynamic duo" in action came to us in one of Maureen's notes to Joanne. Maureen was doing a demonstration at a restaurant in Massachusetts. On her way to the event, she had a visit from Nick. He told her that at the show that night would be a woman whose son had passed in a car accident, and that she would know who the woman was by the number 41.

Maureen was delighted to receive this information, and when she stepped on stage that night, she immediately began looking for a 41. She scanned the room for someone who might be wearing some jewelry, maybe a pin or a shirt with a 41. No luck. She started searching the tables for a card that might read Table #41. No go.

The restaurant where Maureen was appearing was a beautiful venue with huge windows that went from floor to ceiling. It was through those windows that Maureen found her 41. As she continued to scan the audience, Maureen's eye was drawn to one of the cars in the parking lot. The car's license plate was lined up right behind the head of a woman who sat at a table by the window. The woman's head blocked part of the plate, but the part that Maureen could see read 141. Maureen approached the woman and asked if she had lost a son in a car accident.

The woman's reply was, "Oh, my God! Yes, I did!" Maureen went on to bring the boy through, bringing great comfort to the woman.

About six months after Maureen's restaurant appearance, Jean Rondeau invited Joanne and me for a boat ride on Rhode Island's beautiful Narragansett Bay. Jean had invited two other guests, Chris Bouley, president of the Stadium Theatre; and Cathy Levesque Gilbert, the marketing director. It was a beautiful day to be on the water, and while we were making our way through the waves, the topic soon turned to "41." Chris and Cathy had heard a few of the stories, but they both wanted to know more.

I started by recounting the tale of how Jean became a believer after seeing that license plate. I kidded him a little about that license plate being "the straw that broke the camel's back," when it came to bringing him into the fold.

Then I began to tell Chris and Cathy about Maureen's restaurant experience. Meanwhile Jean was dutifully at the helm of his boat, sort of half listening. But when I got to the part of the story where Maureen saw that license plate, I added that, after reading the woman, Maureen noticed that the full number on the plate she saw through the window was XO-141.

In an instant, Jean spun around.

"Hey! That's the same plate I saw at the Stadium that night!"

I only mentioned what the entire number was on the plate Maureen saw because X and O are the symbols for a kiss and a hug. At least that's why I *thought* I mentioned it. But after hearing Jean's amazed reaction, I'm not so sure!

-23-
'Don't Cry Tonight'

Not every story in this book involves the number 41. We've had many other signs to remind us that Nick is always around. Some signs aren't as obvious as others, at least not to me.

About three months after the fire, I took a job as a radio talk-show host for WSAR in Fall River, Massachusetts. Part of the preparation for my show was meeting with some of the support staff. One of these was Production Director Jeff Wite, whose job was to supply some of the production elements for my show.

Jeff asked me what kind of "bump music" I wanted. "Bumps" are the short pieces of music that lead in or out of commercial breaks. Bump music is very important. It's used to set the mood for a show, or it can convey a feeling either for the subject being discussed or the overall sound of the show itself.

Since I was hired for mid-mornings, I asked Jeff to keep it light. I told him that I wanted to stick to music from the '50s and early '60s. I've always had a good feeling about the upbeat sound of the songs from that era. Having this kind of sound has always put me and my audience in a more positive mood.

After that meeting with Jeff, I didn't see him before I started on the air the next Monday morning. Everything went well on that first show. The bumps Jeff chose were just what I wanted. I slid in and out of every break with the sounds of the Beach Boys, Martha and the

Vandellas, Chuck Berry, Buddy Holly and more. It sounded great.

But while coming out of a break during my last hour on the air, I heard a song I didn't recognize. It really threw me. It certainly wasn't a "classic oldie." Oh, it sounded familiar alright, and it was very nice, but it just wasn't what I'd requested.

When I got off the air at noon, Jeff had already gone to lunch, so I couldn't ask him what the deal was with that song. I decided to ask him the next morning. On my drive home I kept thinking about that song. I wasn't upset or angry; it made me chuckle a little: "What was this guy thinking?" After all, he'd done such a good job picking just the right bump music before that song.

With the fire so recent, Joanne still wasn't up to working, so she had been home listening to my show. When I walked into the house, she was smiling. She came to me and gave me a hug.

"I heard the song. Thank you, baby!"

"What song?" I asked.

"*Don't Cry Tonight!* I didn't think you even knew about it."

"You're right," I said. "I don't! What are you talking about?"

Then Joanne told me about the times she and Nick would be alone, and he would play the guitar and sing. Joanne always asked Nick to play the Axel Rose song *Don't Cry Tonight*, the very same song Jeff had chosen to add to my bump music.

That song was a very special memory for Joanne. It must have been special for Nick, too, because he and Joanne got to share it again. And this time, they let me share it too.

-24-
The Music Box

When I started thinking about it, I couldn't decide what the worst day is after someone you love passes. I thought maybe it was the first Christmas or the first birthday, or it might be the day of the first family picnic. Then I decided: It's all of them. Every day is bad, and the special days are worse.

Joanne experienced her first worst day three months after Nick passed. It was Mother's Day 2003. Don't misunderstand. Joanne wasn't mourning Nick to the exclusion of her other sons; not at all. As a matter of fact, she got calls, cards and gifts from the boys that day, and she reveled in their love and attention.

Another difficult aspect of these "worst" days is trying to pick out the right gift. Friends and family flounder, looking for something in good taste. I guess that if you think about it long enough, you can come up with something appropriate. But it can be really tough.

That's why, after going store to store, Nick's oldest brother, Chris, realized that he didn't want something that looked new and mass produced. He wanted something with character and charm. So Chris finally decided to search the flea markets. At his first stop, he was surprised to hear the sound track from the musical *Carousel* playing on the sound system. Hearing those songs reminded Chris of Nick's eerie connection with that musical. It was then that Chris spotted it. Sitting on a table, partially blocked by some less attractive items, was a small, brightly colored music box with a beautifully painted carousel horse mounted on a golden pole.

Chris picked it up; it was just what he was looking for. He turned the key and listened while the carousel horse played a beautiful waltz with those classic music-box chimes. As it wound down and the music came to an end, Chris knew he had found the perfect gift.

On Mother's Day morning, Chris gave Joanne her present. When she opened it, her eyes glistened and her face beamed. She couldn't believe that Chris had found such a wonderful gift. She gently turned the key and smiled while the music played. When it ended, there were several moments of silence. Joanne put her cherished gift in a place of great prominence, on the top of her grandmother's hope chest, next to the pictures of Nick.

I could see how touched Joanne was by Chris's thoughtfulness. Secretly, though, I could almost hear her thinking, "If I could only hear from Nick!"

That night Joanne and I were talking in the bedroom. Chris was in the living room having a snack, sitting directly across from the hope chest. Suddenly, we heard Chris shout: "Mom, come quick, come quick!"

We ran into the living room and saw Chris with eyes as big as saucers. He was staring at the music box, which had suddenly started to play. That's right. This key-wound music box, that had been silent for at least twelve hours, had begun to play again, all by itself. When we realized that Chris hadn't wound it, we were pretty shocked ourselves. But there it was, playing loud and clear.

So Joanne *did* hear from Nick on that Mother's Day after all. You see, Joanne's present, that beautiful, key-wound music box, began playing at exactly 9:41 p.m.

-25-
Billy's Story

Nick isn't the only member of the family with musical talent. His older brother Bill is a singer, and I mean a singer. Bill has a rich, vibrant bass voice. When Bill sings, you need only close your eyes and listen to be transported to another time and place. Bill has performed in operas, musicals, comedies, reviews and solo.

But Bill doesn't just sing. He's had a good deal of success in other facets of the music business. Bill has worked as a pastoral musician, directing choirs and leading choral support for many important religious ceremonies and celebrations. He has also produced and directed children's theater productions for many years. He even did a brief stint as a singing waiter.

Bill's passions include learning. Whether it's music or his avocation, culinary arts, another area where he excels, Bill has always worked toward expanding his abilities. So when Bill told us he had decided to go back to school full time, we really weren't surprised.

After doing his research, Bill narrowed his choices to two schools, the Hartt School of Music in Connecticut and the San Francisco Conservatory of Music (SFC). There were still several details to work out, not the least of which was financial aid. Although Bill was a hard worker, full-time students have a heavy load. Even with his wife, Maureen, working two jobs, making it through school wasn't going to be easy.

After checking out Hartt, Bill decided to make a trip to the West Coast to take a look at SFC. He was already leaning toward the latter, but he still wasn't quite sure. We now realize that somebody else was.

On Bill's first night in San Francisco, he went out to dinner at Max's Opera Café. This restaurant features waiters and waitresses who not only serve, but sing. For Bill, Max's brought back memories of the many nights he had worked as a singing waiter at the Macaroni Grill in Rhode Island. While Bill waited for a seat, he noticed a bus as it passed the restaurant. The bus number was 41. Bill checked his watch. It was 7:41. They called his name, and he was seated at table 41. When the check came, the number on the top of it was 41.

The next morning, while sitting in the lobby at SFC, Bill noticed a display of the proposed building plans for the school's renovation, which called for the addition of new rooms. The list of improvements showed that there would be 41 practice rooms, 41 studios, and an expanded recording studio whose new size would be 411 square feet. While looking over the application paperwork from the conservatory, Bill realized that the San Francisco area code is 415, and the zip code begins with 941, Nick's favorite number. Then he remembered that *Full House*, one of Nick's favorite sitcoms, was set in San Francisco.

Bill was beginning to get the message.

After touring the school, meeting the staff and some of the students, Bill was really excited about the prospect of attending SFC. He was convinced that it was Nick's choice, too. Now the only hurdle left was the money. Well, just six weeks after his visit to SFC, Bill was offered a partial scholarship and a generous aid package.

After getting his "41" signs and receiving the financial assistance he really needed, William Joseph O'Neill enrolled as a full-time student at the San Francisco Conservatory of Music.

Nice job, Nick!

-26-
Cable Channel 41

The interesting thing about the "41s" is that many times they appear in ways you wouldn't expect. The incidents are diverse and unusual. More than once, after experiencing one of these events, I've said to myself, "Who would have thought of doing it that way?"

Our friends Jon Land and Cindy Gilman met each other through their connection with Nick. Jon had heard about Cindy's mediumistic abilities and her visit from Nick. So he was anxious to have a personal reading from her. Cindy and Jon hit it off right away. They have become great friends.

One night Jon invited us out to dinner. Cindy would come along, and we would go to her place afterward for coffee and dessert. What Cindy didn't know was that Jon had a gift for her. A very generous guy, Jon had heard that Cindy's VCR had broken, and he'd bought her a new one.

We met at the restaurant, had a super meal and a great time. When we got to Cindy's, Jon sprang his surprise and began setting up Cindy's new VCR. Since we knew about Jon's plan, we had brought a tape of one of Nick's performances.

Cindy had never met Nick before he passed, only seen some photos of him. Cindy was excited about finally getting to see her friendly spirit in the flesh, albeit on videotape. The tape was of Nick's guest appearance on a local cable show, hosted by Don Lincoln. The show spotlighted local bands. On this show, Nick and his band, Shryne, were the featured guests for the whole hour.

We all sat around Cindy's living room having dessert and watching Nick sing, dance, mug and totally entertain the studio audience. Cindy was mesmerized. She couldn't take her eyes off the young man whom she knew so well but had never seen, at least not like this. Between every song, Nick would introduce a band member, talk about the songs, or just joke around with the crowd.

Then Nick mentioned Eric Leja. Eric was a friend of Nick's who had passed in a car accident just about a year earlier. Nick was dedicating a song to Eric. During the dedication, Nick said, "I know that Eric is up there looking down on us, and that one day Eric and I will be up there together, playing Rock and Roll with C.C. Deville."

At that moment, the tape counter on Cindy's brand new VCR turned to 41. If you ask me, that was cool enough, but the story doesn't stop there.

More than a year later, we were producing *41 the Movie*, and Christian DeRezendes asked me if I could get a clean copy of Don Lincoln's show. We had taped our copy directly from television, so it was of poor quality. Christian needed a copy with better video.

After much wrangling and several phone calls, I got hold of the show on DVD. The picture was much clearer, and Nick looked terrific. When Nick got to the part where he talked about being "up there" playing music with Eric Leja, the number 41:42 popped up on the lower right corner of the screen, then disappeared.

You see, the DVD was a dub from a video tape, and for some reason the counter on the tape suddenly popped up on the DVD, showing a 41 at the moment Nick began talking about himself and Eric being together one day.

I believe what Nick said. I believe that he and Eric are playing their music together, and I bet they sound great!

-27-
Spirit Orbs

How many times have you wished that you could see a loved one who passed…just one more time? Well, you can…in a photo. I'm not talking about old photos. I'm talking about pictures that were taken after they passed. You may think I've finally "lost it," but it's true.

It all started for us when we began noticing spots on some of our photos. These spots looked like drops of dried milk. They were round and grayish. At first I thought that we had spilled something on the photos. But these drops were on several pictures, and were almost uniform in their shape and size.

Our friend, medium Cindy Gilman, enlightened us about this phenomenon. These "spots" are called "spirit orbs," bursts of spirit energy usually not seen by the naked eye. But they can be captured by cameras, particularly digital cameras. Cindy explained that these are actual spirits. They are a life consciousness showing itself as a ball of energy.

About seven months after Nick's passing, Joanne was invited to attend the wedding of one of Nick's closest friends, Adam Pettis and his fiancée, Cathy Pettit. Adam was always very close to our family, so much so that when it came time for the groom to dance with his mother, Adam had two dances: one with his own mom and one with Nick's.

At the wedding of Nick's good friends Adam and Cathy Pettis, Adam dances with Joanne, Nick's mom. A "spirit orb" appears prominently in back of Adam.

As at all weddings, there were heaps of photos taken. There were photos of the ushers and best man, the wedding party seated at the head table, and lots of photos of Adam's dance with Joanne. There was certainly no shortage of wedding pictures and no shortage of "spirit orbs."

You see, Nick was supposed to have been an usher in the wedding party, but he passed before that day came. Still, Adam and Cathy were determined that Nick would be part of their special day. So they set a place for Nick at the head table, and in the picture of the head table, there's an orb at Nick's empty seat. When the ushers lined up for a photo, they left room for Nick to stand. In the picture, you can see an orb in the space left for Nick.

But the best picture was of Adam's dance with Joanne. This photo of the two of them dancing shows an orb sitting prominently on the back of Adam's jacket.

So Nick was at the wedding. He was an usher. He sat at the head table. He even got to share a dance with his mom! And we can prove it because it's all right here in our photo album.

-28-
Meet the Ginsbergs

In April 2004 Joanne signed us up to attend a retreat in the Bahamas, offered by our friend the international medium Robert Brown. Once a year, Robert gathers with a special group of friends and colleagues for a week at the Xanadu Resort in Freeport. All week long these very talented mediums offer demonstrations, classes and lectures on spiritual phenomena.

So Joanne and I, along with roughly thirty other couples, got a chance to spend "quality time" with these gifted souls. We also got to meet other people who believe what we believe: That no one ever dies. I don't think I can express in words just how exciting this experience was!

One of the couples we met on our first day were the Ginsbergs. Bob and Phran are parents of the beautiful and gregarious Bailey, who was just fifteen when she passed in a car accident only a mile from the Ginsberg home. It's amazing how quickly parents who have lost a child seem to bond. The four of us hit it off right away.

We shared photos and stories about how our children passed. But most of all we talked. We had so much in common that we found ourselves almost finishing each other's sentences. The time spent with the Ginsbergs was reassuring and comforting. We felt a real bond with our new friends after they told us a very important story.

On the day of her funeral, Bailey's best friend, Allison, came to the house and told Bob and Phran of a very significant happening. When Bailey and Allison were only twelve, they had made a pact with each other that if either one was to die, she would send a sign to the other that she was okay. Bailey chose a very ambitious sign indeed. She would put a blue Magic Marker in a place where Allison would not expect to find one.

Well, when Ali came home from Bailey's funeral, there on the keyboard of her computer was a blue Magic Marker.

After listening to Bob and Phran tell us about their beautiful daughter and the sign she sent to her friend, Joanne and I both thought that if she and Nick had known one another they would have been great friends. What we didn't consider was that they might already be great friends.

The activities that week included a variety of workshops. Couples were separated so they could have different experiences each day. At the end of each workshop or demonstration, the medium in charge would usually offer to do sittings for the group. This meant that everyone in attendance would be given the opportunity to receive a message or sign from a loved one who had passed.

On our second day there, Joanne was assigned to the Robert Brown group. During the meeting, Robert lectured on proper mediumship, and offered tips and instructions on how they could develop their own abilities. Robert is a fascinating speaker. His stories are always interesting, and his English accent and dry English wit make his talks even more enjoyable.

Near the end of the session Robert began to tell those assembled what messages he was receiving. Joanne and Phran Ginsberg were sitting together in the front row. When Robert came to Joanne, he began describing Nick. He talked about Nick's long hair and imitated Nick's gait while he carried his guitar case. Robert went on for several minutes, and he was accurate with every observation.

Then Robert turned to Phran and said, "And your daughter is with him. She just said to him, "Good job, Nick!"

"Oh, Nick!" Robert said, as he turned to Joanne. "Is that his name, Nick?" Phran and Joanne were thrilled. Imagine, these two women had just met, and already their children were coming through together.

After we got home from the retreat, Bob and I would e-mail or call each other now and again just to keep in touch. I like Bob. He

41 SIGNS of HOPE

and I have the same sense of humor. We always make each other laugh: no one else, just each other.

In June Joanne and I were packing for our move to a new house. I was in my office, and Joanne was putting some of Nick's things in a plastic storage box. I had just gotten an e-mail from Bob Ginsberg, and I was about to call him. But before I could dial his number, Joanne told me she wanted to show me something in Nick's room. When I went into his room, Joanne was smiling and pointing at the storage box she had been filling. Joanne told me that she had been packing items in the box, then closing it. Then she would find another item, open the box, deposit the item, and close the box again. But last time she had opened the box, there inside was a blue Magic Marker! I don't need to tell you that Joanne did not put that marker in the box. But there it was nonetheless!

Now I *really* needed to call Bob.-- When I told him what had just happened, I could hear the smile in his voice. Then he said, "Now let me tell *you* a story." Bob reminded me that Bailey's car accident happened just a mile away from their home and that they had to drive past the site every day. Bob also told me that the crash occurred in front of a historical home. For all the times he passed that spot, he never noticed until the day before our conversation that the number in front of the house was 41.

That was it for me. After hearing that story, I knew that Bailey and Nick were not just friends. They were co-conspirators!

-29-
Tea Time

Nick loved Paris. No, not the city. His Godmother, Paris Ledoux. Paris has always had a sweet, quiet, gentle way about her. She is thoughtful and kind. As a matter of fact, if you were casting a movie and wanted to fill the part of a Godmother, you would give Paris the part.

Paris has two children of her own, Michelle and Michael, whom they called "Mo." Our two families were very close, and Paris and the kids visited often. To Nick's delight, many visits would turn into marathon get-togethers. After several hours, Michelle and Mo would tire and complain that they wanted to go home. Paris would tell them that she was just going to have a cup of tea, and then they would leave. Of course their mom's teacup must have seemed bottomless to Mo and Michelle, because it took forever to empty.

I've observed through the years that most people are not close to their Godparents. Many people I've spoken with about this have actually had to think about who their Godparents were. In fact, in my stand-up act I used to say: If you really didn't like someone, make him or her a Godparent and you will never see them again! Luckily for us, Paris wasn't like that. When it came to her Godson, Paris was always caring and supportive.

About two years after Nick passed, Paris attended a penny social at St. Jude's Church in Lincoln, Rhode Island. Paris is no stranger to

St. Jude's. She has always been an active member, even singing in the choir. When she arrived at the event that night, she bought her tickets and placed them in the cups sitting in front of the prizes.

Poor Paris has never been especially lucky when it comes to raffles. She was really just there to support the church. So when they began to draw tickets and give away prizes, Paris was talking with the other people at her table and not really paying attention. But then she began to get a feeling that her number was going to be called. So she turned and listened.

Then it happened. The MC for the evening reached into the cup, drew the ticket, and read Paris's number. When she went up to get her prize, Paris couldn't believe what she saw. There, taped to a beautifully wrapped basket of tea and tea products, with a tag that read "Tea Time," was the prize number: 41.

That night Paris might have been hoping for a stroke of luck. What she got was a giant basket of love.

-30-
Morse Code

Phran Ginsberg thought her car radio had a problem. She began hearing some "buzzing" in her speakers. At first she thought it might be a short circuit or some kind of outside interference. The sound persisted, and the more Phran heard it the more it sounded like code, Morse Code. The volume never wavered, and the cadence was always the same. She could almost imitate the sound. The mystery continued. Every once in a while the "code" would be heard.

Phran's "Morse Code" never showed up on Bob's radio. That is until Phran's car had to go in for repairs and she had to use Bob's. Then, sure enough, when Phran turned on the radio, there it was, the same sound she had heard on her car radio.

This might be a good time to tell you something else about our friends, the Ginsbergs. Allison's story about the pact the two girls had made, and Bailey's keeping her promise, intrigued Bob and Phran. They wanted to know more, much more. They wanted to find out if this type of thing was really possible. They wanted answers.

Now, Bob Ginsberg was never someone who would readily buy into anything like this. He needed proof. So he began reading and doing all sorts of research. He was determined to find the truth. What he found was that Bailey's story was just one of virtually thousands, maybe millions, of stories that happen every day.

It was then that Bob and Phran decided to start the "Forever Family Foundation." The goal of this foundation is to find and validate indisputable, scientific evidence that our loved ones never die. Bob and Phran were determined to prove, once and for all, that families stay together forever.

One of the people the Ginsbergs were able to recruit in their cause was Dr. Gary E. Schwartz, professor of psychology, surgery, medicine and neurology at the University of Arizona. Gary also is the author of *The Afterlife Experiments*, written for people who long to find a scientific bearing on what they hold most dear: that love matters, that love evolves, and that love continues forever. Discovering the existence of the living soul may be one of humankind's greatest gifts. Gary has been very active in the Forever Family Foundation and has helped make amazing strides in the research of survival of consciousness.

Now back to our story.

I've been referring to the sound on Phran's radio as a code because that's exactly what it sounded like. Phran felt right from the beginning that it was Bailey causing the sound. After dealing with this on her own for some time, Phran called Gary Schwartz. Gary wanted to try an experiment.

He asked Phran to speak with Bailey and ask her to send a message to Janet Mayer, a very gifted medium Gary had been working closely with on several afterlife experiments. The message was to be a simple one, the two words "Morse code." For the sake of validating this experiment, Gary asked Phran not to tell anyone what she was doing and, of course, Gary told no one.

Each night, during her private time with Bailey, Phran would ask her to send the words "Morse code" to Janet Mayer. Phran and Gary had no idea what their little experiment might bring. But still, with faith and hope, Phran did as she was asked, and they both waited.

Then, after just three days, Gary received an e-mail from Janet Mayer saying, "I have a feeling that this is for you. Over and over again someone keeps sending me the words 'Morse code.'"

Morse code is a communication method invented in 1843. This system, developed by Samuel Morse, used keypads to send and receive messages over miles and miles of telegraph wire. I'm not surprised that Bailey would use a similar method, except that Bailey didn't use wires or keypads. She just sent her message of reassurance from one loving heart to another.

-31-
Encore Performer

Nick's time with Encore Repertory Company was very exciting. His brother Chris was with Encore as a director. This meant that Nick and Chris got to work together. I have to tell you that this was a very good arrangement because Chris understood Nick and knew how to handle him.

Remember that Nick, for all his talent, was still a real kid. He loved to mess around. He was always able to find a way to get a laugh. Unfortunately, Nick's antics were not always appreciated by the powers at Encore. To tell you the truth, I didn't blame them. Still, Nick loved being part of Encore, and they were glad to have him.

After Nick passed, the boards of Encore and the Stadium Theatre honored Nick by presenting us with a plaque that would grace the back of one of the chairs in the theater. The Stadium makes these plaques available for people who want to make a donation in someone's name. When donors attend a performance, they can reserve the seat that carries the name of their loved one.

I used to say it was better to reserve the seat behind that chair so you could see your loved one's name when you sat down!

When we received Nick's plaque, no one at Encore knew about the significance of the number 41. Actually, we were just beginning to realize it ourselves. So there was no attempt to place the plaque on seat number 41. As a matter of fact, there is no seat number 41 in the Stadium Theatre. The plaque was placed on a seat completely at random. Or was it?

At "Night of Angels," I was standing on stage welcoming the crowd. In an attempt to loosen up the audience, I asked the person sitting in Nick's seat to stand. I told him that he was sitting in the seat that held the plaque that read "Nick O'Neill Encore Performer." Then I asked him if he wouldn't mind "scooting" over a bit in case Nick wanted to join him. This got a big laugh and a round of applause from the audience.

But it wasn't until I was watching the videotape of that show three weeks later that I realized what had I said. I knew which seat had Nick's plaque, of course, but I didn't realize where it was until I heard myself say, "Would the person sitting in the fourth row, first seat please stand?"

Fourth row, first seat: 4-1.

-32-
Don't Go Changing

It was Sunday morning, November 13, 2005, and I was very tense. In just three hours, five hundred people were going to file into the Stadium Theatre to watch and listen to international medium Robert Brown in a fundraising event for the Nicholas O'Neill Scholarship Fund. Joanne and I had asked Robert if he would come to Rhode Island to give a demonstration and lecture on mediumship. He agreed almost before we could finish asking, and we were very excited.

I have produced, directed and hosted many shows in my career, including stage shows, Santa arrivals, comedy nights, even radio and television specials and documentaries. But, for some reason, I was as tight as a drum before this Robert Brown appearance. Oh, I had all my ducks in a row. The Stadium had done a terrific job promoting Robert's appearance, and we'd had a brisk pre-sale on tickets.

The people we'd depended on so often were there for us again. Dennis Tancrel had arranged for all the audio/visual support at the Stadium. Christian DeRezendes came up from New York to supply the camera work we needed to make this look good. The entire production staff at the theater, all volunteer, was at the ready. I didn't even have to worry about Robert getting into town. He was already there and had come to our home for dinner on Saturday night.

So there was no need for me to be so nervous.

I guess that my tension was beginning to get on Joanne's nerves.

After watching me pace back and forth while I checked and re-checked my list of things to do, she let me have it. Gently – okay, maybe not so gently — Joanne told me that I wasn't showing very much faith. She reminded me that Nick would never let us down, and that it was Robert Brown who had given us the most compelling message we had ever received from our son: "The show must go on."

Joanne's words irritated me, not because she was wrong but because she was very right. I felt foolish worrying about everything. I was even tormenting myself over whether to wear a suit or a sport jacket and slacks. When Joanne finished I grumbled something unintelligible, even to me. I reached into my closet and grabbed the first pair of slacks I saw. As I yanked them off the hanger, I heard change hitting the bedroom floor. I looked down to see a quarter, a dime, a nickel and a penny: 41 cents.

You know, I wrote this book to give encouragement to people. I wrote this book to assure them that their loved ones never die. I wrote this book to remind people that all their worry about everything is really worry about nothing at all. Now that I've written it, maybe I ought to read it!

-33-
Love Letters

The sudden loss of a loved one always seems to bring about the same questions. Why them? Why this way? Why now?

Of course the "whys" are mostly rhetorical. The answers to these and a thousand more questions will have to wait until it's our time to pass. Still, there are always doubts. You wonder if you did enough. You may even fantasize about being able to go back and do it all again.

You know, when we leave our friends and family, we actually take for granted that we will see them again. We say, "talk to you later," "see you tomorrow," "I'll meet you at the gym on Tuesday." It just doesn't occur to us that we may be spending our last earthly moments with that person. We always think that we have plenty of time. Oh, we plan to say nice things; we just try to pick the perfect time, as if we knew the perfect time. We wait for a birthday, anniversary or retirement party. Sometimes we're motivated to say something when a close friend or relative falls ill. The truth is that the perfect time is like tomorrow: It never comes.

One night shortly after Nick passed, I was in a very down and doubtful mood. I sat on the couch wondering if I had said enough to Nick about how much I love him. I tormented myself over the thought that I had let too much time go by without reminding him how much he meant to me. Over and over again I tried to remember the times I encouraged him. I just wanted to be sure.

While I sat there, wiping my eyes, Joanne came into the living room holding a piece of paper.

"Hey, look what I've got," she said.

I took the paper and began to read. It was a letter she'd found in her dresser drawer, a letter I'd written to Nick at Christmas just two years earlier. Here were all the words and phrases I had just told myself I would have said to Nick if I had another chance. The letter said how much he meant to me and reminded him of how proud I was of him, not for what he had done, but just because he was who he was.

I couldn't believe it!

Here was the reassurance I needed so desperately, proof that every word I wanted to tell Nick was already written in this special Christmas letter. And that wasn't the only correspondence we received that year.

If you ask anyone who has had a loss, they'll tell you that holidays are the saddest times. In an attempt to make it through, Joanne would start some project. A few weeks before Easter, for example, she was trying to find a cookbook for Chris. She didn't want anything fancy, just a book with the basics. Unfortunately, Joanne didn't have much luck. After searching through bookstores, she decided instead to give Chris one of her own cookbooks.

On the night before Easter, Joanne went into the kitchen and opened a drawer as she had done a hundred times that week. But this time she saw a piece of paper on top of the cookbooks. Joanne picked up the paper and immediately recognized the handwriting.

It was Nick's.

The paper was a letter from Nick, written to her on Easter a year earlier, a love note to his mom, full of warmth and devotion. It was a letter that told her just how much her son loved and treasured her, and it was signed simply, "I love you, xoxo, Nick."

It's a funny thing about letters. Sometimes you send one and the person you wrote to never gets it. At other times you get someone else's mail. But not letters like the one Joanne found. Letters like that are in a very different category.

You see, that year we were living in a condo while we were between houses. The condo was very small. So until the new house was ready, most of the furniture and all the other non-essential possessions were placed in storage. And that's exactly where those letters would have been: in storage. We wouldn't have brought a letter from two Christmases before and an Easter letter from the previous year with us to such a small place.

No, sir, we didn't bring those letters with us. They came special delivery.

-34-
It's a Date!

It has taken me almost three years to realize my dream of making *41 Signs of Hope* a reality. I started writing it about six months after Nick passed. At the same time, I was searching for a publisher. Anyone who has ever attempted to become a published author will tell you just how difficult that is.

You'd think that with the size of the book market today, publishing houses would be begging for new manuscripts. Not so. Publishers are very picky, which to me is surprising, considering the number of books that I wouldn't even use as doorstops. Nonetheless I had a very tough time interesting anyone in my manuscript.

Briefly I considered "self-publishing." That basically means that you hire a printer to produce your book, then you have the job of trying to sell enough of them to make your money back. But if you have a strong belief in your topic and you have faith that others will too, then you have a shot at breaking even. Of course, with most people who decide to self-publish, the money isn't important, only telling the story matters.

I had just begun to write my book when I was introduced to Cate Monroe, owner of Moon Mountain Press. Moon Mountain was a one-woman shop. Cate was the manager, the editor, and the promotion and sales person. She did it all. Cate was very gracious and agreed to look at the stories I had written. A few weeks later, she e-mailed me and said how much she liked what I had sent her. But, with Moon Mountain publishing mostly illustrated children's titles, she wasn't sure that she was the best person to do this type of book.

I'd already learned that when you hear that from a publisher, it's usually their way of passing on your book. Not so with Cate. She offered to help me in any way she could. She looked over my work and encouraged me with every correspondence. Unfortunately, Moon Mountain Press went the way of so many small businesses, and Cate had to close up shop. Cate's call letting me know her decision seemed a bit lopsided to me. She sounded almost apologetic, saying how sorry she was that she wouldn't be able to publish my book.

"But I'll do anything I can to assist your search for a publisher. I believe in what you're doing, and I want to help."

When I hung up the phone I wasn't just disappointed. I was sad. I liked Cate. I had a good feeling about her. She was genuine, and I needed someone like that to accomplish my goal.

About two days after Cate's call, I decided that I really needed to get busy finding another publisher. I planted myself at the computer and opened my e-mail. There was a note from Cate. It said simply, "Do you know about these people?" She had sent me the web address for New River Press, a small, family-owned publishing business located barely a mile from the Stadium Theatre. Well, you're reading the book, so you already know that New River Press published it. But here's what you don't know.

I contacted New River's president, Paul Eno. Paul not only heads his family's publishing operation, he's a prize-winning newspaperman and the author of several books of his own. I think this has given him much better insight into what makes a good book. In an amazing irony, Paul also is an internationally known expert and speaker on the paranormal. With thirty-five years of experience under his belt, he's one of the world's most experienced "ghost hunters." He had an immediate appreciation for Nick and our "41" experiences.

After looking over the samples I sent, Paul invited Joanne and me to lunch. As soon as we met him, we immediately knew that we had found our publisher. Paul displayed a real understanding for the material, grasped what I was trying to do, and he wanted to be part of it. As we walked to the parking lot after our luncheon meeting, Joanne said, "I like that man." I said, "me too," and we signed the deal.

Feelings are so important, aren't they? It's important to me that I do business with people I like. I try to have people around me whom I know I can trust. I think this is important, especially in a writer/ publisher relationship. The writer has to put so much trust in the publisher's expertise, and the publisher has to trust that the author has the ability to deliver a good product.

Well, I was comfortable, very comfortable. And I guess I wasn't the only one.

The only stipulation I insisted on in our contract was that this book be on the shelves no later than mid-February 2006. This was very important. You see, I wanted the book out in time for the third anniversary of The Station nightclub fire: February 20, 2006. Paul, of course, agreed and got right to work.

In less than two weeks he and the New River Press crew (mostly Paul's immediate family and cousins involved in the business) had really done a lot. There was a website (41signsofhope.com), publicity had begun, and he had assigned an editor to work on the material. I was sure that Paul was going to keep his promise to have my book on the shelves by mid-February. I was very pleased.

Then, one day not long after everything was in the works, I decided to see if I was famous yet. I did something silly, just for fun. I "googled" the name of my book, and "voila": There it was — *41 Signs of Hope* right on the Barnes and Noble website. What a kick! I couldn't believe it!

As I re-read the ad for my book, I realized that Barnes and Noble was offering *41 Signs of Hope* as "Available for Pre-Order. This item will be available on January 28, 2006."

Isn't that cool? Paul didn't even know that. Barnes and Noble certainly didn't know that. Isn't what cool? Oh, I'm sorry! You didn't know either. January 28th is Nick's Birthday!

-35-
Pro Wrestler

Shortly after "Night of Angels," Nick's pal Matt DeThomas returned to his college, Suffolk University in Massachusetts. On one of his first days back, Matt was in one of his communications classes. That day the class was to view a documentary entitled *Wrestling with Manhood*, a video about live professional wrestling and the people who follow it.

As the video began, Matt wasn't particularly interested. He was tired and wasn't paying much attention — that is until he saw a familiar face on the screen. Matt sat bolt upright in his seat. I think it's safe to say that the rest of the class sat up as well when they heard Matt's rather loud and enthusiastic, "Holy Shit!"

The face on the screen was Nick's.

There he was, big as life, being interviewed about his interest in World Wrestling Entertainment (WWE). Nick and his buddy Tom Kane had been stopped by the interviewer and asked a few questions. Nick was priceless, mugging and making jokes. This clip was a perfect example of the kind of zest Nick showed for life every day.

Immediately after class Matt hunted down the name of the company that produced the film. Then he called Nick's brother Chris, who called his mom. I followed up with a call to the producer of the documentary. This was a difficult call for me to make. Not only did

I have to explain why I was so interested in the video, but I didn't even know how long ago this show had been done. Although I vaguely remembered Nick saying something about being interviewed when he went to the Providence Civic Center for a WWE event, I couldn't be more specific than that.

When I finally got hold of the producer, she couldn't have been nicer. She told me that she actually remembered Nick and not only offered to send us *Wrestling with Manhood*, but the raw footage of Nick and Tom as well. She expressed her condolences and promised to send everything out that day. I couldn't wait!

The package arrived in less than a week. I tore open the mailing envelope and popped the tape into the VCR. It began with opening credits, music, clips from the WWE and shots of an audience full of screaming fans. Then we saw him. Nick and Tom appeared on our screen at exactly 2:41.

-36-
The Graduate

Joanne and I were pretty much in agreement when it came to raising Nick. He was a typical kid, and he had his moments, like most kids, but he was a really good boy. I used to wonder if he ever just "chilled out." He never stopped: He was always laughing, mugging, jumping on his bed or a couch, and generally living life for all it was worth.

But Nick hated school. Oh, not all school. He liked elementary school and, for awhile, we had him in a Catholic school. He liked it there, which I found odd. You'd think that someone with Nick's exuberance would have a problem with such a disciplined structure, but he did well. But when he got into his teenage years, Nick's feelings began to change. He left the Catholic school and attended a public high school. If you've ever tried to make that transition from private to public school, you know what a culture shock it can be. Well, to Nick it was more like an electric shock. He hated it.

Nick stuck it out, but it was a real struggle. The closer he got to sixteen, the legal age for quitting school, the more the subject came up. Nick wanted out. But I felt an important obligation as his dad to see to it that he graduated. I wanted him to have at least a high school diploma.

Joanne's take was to consider home schooling Nick. She felt that the school was horrible, and with Nick hating it the way he did, Joanne wanted to come to his rescue. I didn't have a problem with this, except that Joanne's plate was already filled. She ran a daycare service in the house all day. I was concerned that Nick wouldn't take the home schooling seriously, and I worried about Joanne being overworked.

Eventually we all decided that Nick could quit school. Our plan was to get him his GED. Then he could enroll at a junior college and eventually get a college degree. At least that was the plan. Nick was tested for his GED and, as it turned out, he needed only one math course to pass. I actually took him to start his math class. But, for some reason, the class was cancelled that night and, as things turned out, Nick never got to go back.

Nick dropping out of school really bothered me. I'm certainly not the world's best dad, but I really felt that I should be sure he graduated. I've always had butterflies in my stomach when I think about this decision. I remember thinking that I had really let him down. It drove me nuts.

Joanne also felt bad about it, thinking that she should have home schooled Nick as soon as he displayed such a deep dislike for the high school. Joanne and I discussed all these regrets several times, even after Nick passed.

Just a week after our last discussion about this, Nick's brother Billy was in town, and we all decided to go for a sitting with Cindy Gilman. During the sitting Cindy asked, "Who's the fat, bald guy?"

Joanne and I laughed. I raised my hand while she pointed at me. Nick had a name for me: "The Fat Old Bald Bastard." I told Cindy that this was meant very respectfully, of course, and was used only when I wasn't around. Cindy laughed out loud. Then she said, "Okay, I get that. But why does he keep showing himself to me in a cap and gown?"

Wow, I guess there's more than one way to graduate! Eh, Nick?

-37-
Your Lucky Number

One night Joanne and I were driving to a show and talking about all the moving experiences we'd had with mediums, who have played a huge part in our journey since Nick passed.

I know that for many people the jury is still out as to whether mediums are for real. Certainly, as in any other sector of life, there are incompetents and charlatans, and I can understand the tendency of people to be skeptical. But I have to tell you that when it comes to the gifted individuals who have assisted us with our connection with Nick, Cindy Gilman, Robert Brown, Maureen Hancock and Roland Comtois, we're convinced that it's all very real.

We were also well aware that people who loved and cared about us worried about our ability to deal with our grief. We know that some of our closest friends believed, at first, that we were "grasping at straws" when we began to tell them about our signs from Nick. I don't blame them. I had more than a little trouble understanding all the things that were happening too.

While we moved along the highway, Joanne was talking about the indisputable messages and experiences we received during our sittings. You've already read about Nick's visit to Cindy Gilman the day after the fire. It was this visit that started it all for us. And of course there was the message that Robert Brown gave us from Nick, "The show must go on." These were the last words Nick spoke to me on the day before the fire.

But we weren't the only people to get absolute proof that these mediums were genuine. Nick's brother Chris wanted desperately to know that he was really connecting with Nick. So when he was on his way to a sitting with our friend Cindy Gilman, Chris prayed silently, "Nick, if this is really you, send me a 'Calvin and Hobbes' reference."

"Calvin and Hobbes" is a comic strip that features two charming characters, a little boy with a hat made out of a folded section of the Sunday newspaper, and his companion, a talking stuffed tiger. On so many nights when they were both much younger, Chris would read "Calvin and Hobbes" to Nick as he sat in Chris's lap. The boys both treasured this time together, and Chris knew that if Cindy mentioned "Calvin and Hobbes" it would be undeniable proof that Nick was checking in.

But Cindy never mentioned Calvin and Hobbes. She obviously had never heard of the comic strip, because in the middle of their sitting she paused, gave Chris a quizzical look and asked, "Why is Nick wearing a newspaper hat?"

Chris was stunned and delighted. He had told no one about his deal with Nick, yet there he was letting Chris know that it was really him. But the story doesn't end there.

You see, all through this book we've talked about Nick's special number, 41. But Chris has a special number too, 711. Chris was born at eleven minutes after seven in the evening, and he weighed seven pounds, eleven ounces.

"Why do I need to know that?" you may ask.

Because while Joanne and I were driving and talking about Chris's sign from Nick, the time they spent together, and the wonderful bond they shared, a car passed us. The license number on that car was 71141.

-38-
That's What You Think

We had arranged to bring Robert Brown in to do a fundraiser for Nick's scholarship fund. I was sure we had thought of everything. I even thought of a way to present his demonstration, without the problems these types of programs always have.

You see, when a medium does a demonstration, it's usually in a meeting room or auditorium. The medium stands before the crowd and, after speaking for a while and answering some questions, he or she begins to give whatever messages are received. The problem comes when the message is for someone sitting in the middle or back of the audience.

If the other people are sitting near the front of the room and want to see the person getting the message, they need to crank their necks around. If the person being read is near the front of the audience, those behind can't see anything but his or her back. This can be uncomfortable and distracting, but I thought I had a solution.

Instead of having everyone stretching to see the person receiving a message, I thought we would do something different. I asked Christian DeRezendes to set up his camera on stage next to Robert Brown. Using a spotlight, the camera, wireless microphones and a video projector, the audience would be able to see Robert on stage and the person he was talking to on the big screen behind him.

When we were planning for this, Christian asked me if I wanted to tape the event. I said I didn't think so, since we weren't going to use this for anything.

"I think I'll just pop in a tape. You never know," Christian responded.

I should tell you that this presentation worked wonderfully! The whole audience could see everything without being uncomfortable or missing out.

Robert's last message that day was for someone right in the middle of the audience. As he pointed to the center of the orchestra seating, he said, "I have a young man who passed from a car accident, right here."

A young lady with blond hair raised her hand. Robert told her that this young man had a message for someone who was supposed to be with her that day. The person Robert was talking about was the young man's mother. Robert told this woman the messages that the young man had for her, including the most important of all. He wanted to tell his mom that he felt no pain when it happened, that it had been over in an instant.

Then Robert told the audience and the woman he was speaking with that the young man wanted to let the person who was driving the car that hit him know that he forgave him.

Forgiveness: What a wonderful and important message, but it wasn't until the next day that I realized how important it was. On Monday, the day after Robert Brown's appearance, I got a call from Cathy Levesque Gilbert, the Stadium Theatre's marketing director. She told me about a call she had just received from the mother of that young man. She wanted to know if there was any way she could get a tape of the show. Cathy didn't know if we had taped that day, so she said she would check with me.

Cathy gave me the woman's number, and I called her right away. Her name was Pat. Her son's name was Louis. Pat's journey after Louis' passing had been a rough one. She had experienced what many might call a "crisis of faith." But through some amazing happenings and a few messages that Pat had gotten directly from Louis, she was finding her way back.

Pat told me that the driver's name was Scott. He was just a young man himself, only twenty seven. The accident had certainly taken quite a toll on him as well. Since that day Scott had been suffering from severe depression. There had even been rumors of failed suicide attempts. Pat knew that if her healing was to be complete, she had to do what she could for Scott.

That's why Pat wanted the tape. She wanted to bring it to Scott so he could see for himself that Louis had forgiven him.

So you see, I thought I knew why I wanted to have a camera at the Robert Brown event. Christian thought he knew why he wanted to tape it, just in case. But the truth is that other forces directed all this. I think that Nick and Louis have met each other. I think Louis wanted to help his mom and Scott, and Nick wanted to help Louis. So they devised this way to do it.

What do you think?

Pat has written a book about her own road to recovery: *Healing Life's Broken Dreams*. On the prologue page is the date November 23, 1998, the day her son Louis was hit by the car. Joanne and I delivered the DVD to Pat on November 23, 2005. We didn't realize the significance of that date until we read Pat's book.

Now what do you think?

-39-
Joseph

In March 2005 we entered Nick's play-turned-movie *They Walk Among Us* in the Black Point Film Festival in Lake Geneva, Wisconsin. It was a very gutsy move on our part. We had never done anything like this before, and we were really anxious to see how the film would do.

We hadn't done this before, but Christian DeRezendes had. Christian was the production wizard behind *They Walk Among Us*. He had lots of experience in the independent film world, and he was the man behind *Getting Out of Providence* and many other independent film projects. Actually it was Christian who decided we should enter the competition.

Christian has always had faith in Nick's play. His devotion and hard work, along with the direction by Nick's brother Chris, made the film what it was: moving, inspirational and uplifting. Still, when we looked at all the other entries there would be, we could do little more than pray and keep our fingers crossed.

At the same time that year, Chris was directing *Joseph and the Amazing Technicolor Dream Coat* for the Encore Repertory Company at the Stadium Theatre. *Joseph* is a very ambitious undertaking for any director. But for Chris it became an epic. The impressive feature of Chris's productions is his reputation for going full out. Chris has never been interested in just doing a show. He wants to give his audiences a thoroughly enjoyable theatrical experience.

On opening weekend the combination of the *Joseph* play and word that Chris was the director resulted in a near sell-out crowd. On Saturday night there was real excitement in the theater. The cast, some thirty actors strong, was ready, and so was the audience. This was going to be a very special night!

The first act went off without a hitch, and the applause as the curtain came down was thunderous. Chris was feeling great. Everything was going just as he had planned, and even the set looked super. The sound was solid, and he was getting all kinds of compliments during intermission. Yep, Chris was very pleased.

Then the lights went out. And I mean the lights went out: total darkness except for the emergency lights.

Nobody knew what was happening. The theater management called the utility company, and they said there were no blackouts in the central Woonsocket area. They offered to send a truck, but that would take a good hour. If the electricity was off, then continuing with the play was out of the question, so the theater management had to make a decision.

It looked like this night was on its way to being perfect, alright: a perfect disaster.

While the Stadium bigwigs were huddling, Chris was pacing. He kept looking at his watch. The lights went out at 8:30, and Chris had a feeling that if they just waited until 8:41, the lights would come back on. He said nothing; just kept checking his watch. The president of the Stadium Theatre, Chris Bouley, made his way to the stage and tried to get everyone's attention. He began to explain that the show would have to be cancelled.

While the man spoke, Chris's eyes were glued to his watch. He could hear the audience moan at the prospect of having to end this night. As the crowd complained to one another, Chris quietly prayed as the second hand on his watch swept its way past the nine and up to the twelve. Chris began to smile; he just knew what was about to happen. Sure enough, when the second hand was straight up, marking 8:41, every light in the theater came back on!

Pretty good, huh? Well, as they say in those television commercials: "Wait, there's more!"

Just two days later we got the news we had been waiting for. The Black Point Film Festival had announced winners. On that Saturday night, the same night and at the same time the lights went out in the Stadium Theatre in Woonsocket, the Black Point Film Festival in Wisconsin began screening *They Walk Among Us*. Then the official there announced that Nicholas O'Neill had won the "Best Screenplay Award."

I guess Nick just wanted to let his brother know that he wasn't the only one having a good night!

-40-
Only the Beginning

The stories in this book are only the beginning. They haven't stopped. We experience one event after another. Family members and friends call to tell us of unexplained occurrences almost every day. These happenings involve "41s," the date of Nick's birthday, special songs and much more. These are so frequent that I could never keep up or write in depth about them all. But I can't resist giving you at least a thumbnail sketch of some of these other "Signs of Hope."

• In our family albums we found two pictures, both taken before Nick passed. The first includes a wall clock in the kitchen of Nick's house on Wentworth Avenue. The clock reads 4:41. The second picture is of a transom over a door on a building. The number is 541. We don't know who took these pictures or why, and no one seems to remember ever seeing them before.

• Shortly after the fire, I took over Nick's cell phone number. Like most cell phones, mine would beep when someone left me a message. The trouble was that my phone began to beep when there was no message. This happened more and more frequently. I began to feel that it was Nick checking in, because it seemed to beep whenever I would either mention Nick or make a statement that he would agree with.

The best example of this occurred one night when we were all in

41 SIGNS of HOPE

the living room. Chris had just come back from his sitting with Cindy Gilman. At one point during our conversation, I told Chris that he was a terrific brother to Nick. At that moment, my cell phone beeped three times. Yep, Nick agreed.

• Just a few months after the fire, I heard a news report that the band "Great White" had announced a tour to raise funds for victims of The Station nightclub fire. I couldn't decide how I felt about this. After all it was "Great White" performing at The Station that night, and it was their pyrotechnics that started the fire. Part of me wanted them to just go away. The other part of me felt, "Well at least they're attempting to do something."

Nick helped me decide. While I was thinking about it, I heard the reporter say that this would be a 41-city tour for the band.

• Whenever we go out as a group, we always leave a spot for Nick. His Aunt Julie is Joanne's sister. On Julie's birthday we all went out to dinner. Julie is very sensitive to Nick's messages and signs, and we knew he would check in. When the bill came for the dinner that night, the total was $41.41.

• Eric is Julie's son and Nick's cousin. He was very nervous about starting high school. But he felt much better when he was assigned locker number 2041.

• When Eric purchased the ticket for his first high school dance, the ticket number was 141.

• Cara is Eric's sister, and she loves cats. Julie was shopping for clothes one day and found a rack of shirts, but only one had a picture of a cat on it and was Cara's size. Cara tried on her new cat shirt and, in the pocket, she found a slip of paper that read: Inspected by #41.

• In July Cara broke her arm. It was a serious break and there was talk of surgery. While sitting in the hospital waiting room, a feather floated down and landed on Cara. In the examining room, another feather came down, apparently from the ceiling. It was then that the doctor delivered the good news: she wouldn't need the surgery after all.

• While visiting St. Jude's Church one afternoon, Joanne noticed that the posted hymn list included hymn #441. Out of curiosity she picked up a hymnal to see the name of that hymn. Page 441 was dog-eared, but the hymn was *On Eagles Wings*, Joanne's favorite. She knew her boy was checking in.

• Then Joanne went to the market. The man in front of her in the checkout line had a cap with 41 on it. The total for Joanne's order came to $14.

• While shooting *They Walk Among Us*, our friend and lighting director Dennis Tancrel was taking a video of our attempt to get a white feather to land on the lens of Christian DeRezendes's camera. This shot was a climactic moment in the play. With continual attempts, one after another, the uncooperative feather finally landed on its mark. Dennis's video counter showed that the feather landed at exactly 5:41.

• When we moved into the new house, there was a kitchen clock that plugged into a wall outlet. One day the hands of the clock stopped at 3:41. The clock was still running. The pendulum was still moving. Only the hands had stopped. Three days later, the clock's hands began to move again, and it has kept perfect time ever since.

• On Easter Sunday, two years after Nick passed, we were in New York City for a sitting with Robert Brown. We had arrived at the Hilton Hotel the night before. We decided to take a walk to get a peek at Trump Towers, but we got the wrong directions. We turned a corner and there, imbedded in the sidewalk, was a huge brass 41. We looked up, and there was another giant 41 on the face of the building.

• One evening we rented *It's a Wonderful Life*. The first time the angel appeared in the movie, it was 9:41.

• Joanne's employee number at her new job ends in 41.

• Joanne and I were driving to a show on a warm summer's evening, and we were talking about Nick. We passed a bank with a giant time and temperature display. When we drove by, it was frozen at 41 degrees.

• Chris was walking to a deli restaurant in his neighborhood. He was thinking about how many "41s" he had been getting that day. When he walked into the deli, the guy behind the counter was calling "Number 41!"

• St. Jude's Church had a memorial service for all parishioners who had passed that year. During the service, both Julie's and Joanne's cell phones rang at 7:41.

• Leah's cell phone beeped with a message from a friend saying that he was praying for us. The message was sent at 9:41.

• Right after the fire, Gabby, Nick's girlfriend, got a fortune cookie message that read: "You will always be taken care of."

• The weekend after Nick passed, his brother David went out with his buddies and drank too much beer. His kidney backed up, and he was rushed to the hospital. They found a birth defect that no one had known about. Two weeks later David had surgery to repair the problem. When the nurse came out of the operating room to tell us the surgery was over and that David would be fine, it was 4:41 p.m.

• The night before his surgery David was very nervous. He had never even been in a hospital before. He lay awake, unable to sleep. Suddenly there was a huge flash that illuminated the entire room. David looked at his clock. It was 3:41 a.m.

• Gabby and Nick's friend Emily Kunkel were standing in line at a pizza parlor. A little boy and his mother were in front of them. The girls thought that the boy looked just like Nick when he was little. Just then, they heard the boy's mother say, "You'll look just like Nicholas someday."

• Emily and Gabby managed to sneak into Nick's old house while it was still vacant. They looked in a closet and found a store receipt from 1985, the year Nick was born. The receipt said: "41 cents change."

• Nick had several "pet names" for me. One of them was "The Old Sea Captain." We were leaving a restaurant one day, and the waiter said goodbye to Joanne and "so long, Captain" to me. I turned and asked him why he had said that. The reply: "Well, I don't really know. It just popped into my head that you looked like a sea captain!"

• I got to the radio station one morning and saw that the morning's *Providence Journal* had a picture of Nick in The Station nightclub, just minutes before he passed. I called Joanne to warn her. When I hung up, I realized I had called at 9:41.

• Joanne visited the cemetery every day. It always seemed that while she was there, wrens would come around and sing to her. On her way to the cemetery that same morning, Joanne had to pass a newspaper vending box full of *Journals* with Nick's picture on the front page. As she approached, Joanne saw a wren sitting on the box waiting for her.

• A listener to my radio show, who knew nothing about the significance that wrens held for us, decided to send me a picture from her back yard. The picture was of a baby wren peaking out of a birdhouse.

• When Nick created *They Walk Among Us*, the part he wrote for himself was Cyrus the angel. When Gabby attended Walnut Hill, an acting camp for young people, she met a girl who claimed to have the ability to communicate with angels. The girl told Gabby that, just before coming to camp, she had met an angel named Cyrus.

• Nick's Uncle Vito has "41s" all around him. He was the first of several people who got tattoos to honor Nick. Vito's tattoo is a huge "41"with a guitar on a beautiful blue background. This extensive artwork took several hours to accomplish. When it was all over, the clock said 5:41.

• The year Nick passed, I had a heart attack. When we were in the emergency room, I was lying on a gurney and Joanne was holding my hand. We were alone for a few minutes, and she said, "I can feel Nick here. I can almost see him standing right over there." Just as she said that, an IV pole hanging just above the spot Joanne pointed to began to sway back and forth. I looked at my watch, it was 5:41.

• Nick's friend Cathy Pettis wanted to organize a fundraiser for the Nicky O' Foundation. The only week her company could offer her was that of January 28th. January 28th is Nick's birthday.

• The year after he passed, we celebrated Nick's birthday at a restaurant. We stayed there a long time. When we began to leave, we heard a song that has a special meaning to us: Billy Joel's *I Love You Just the Way You Are* began playing at 8:41.

• Two days after the fire, Chris was driving and feeling very low. A fire truck entered the traffic lane in front of him and on the back was the engine's number, a giant E-41.

• Chris is the family archivist. He's always the one with either the video camera or his digital still camera, taking the pictures. When we got home from Walt Disney World, Chris realized that his digital camera had deleted two pictures he had taken. This random deletion left Chris with 41 pictures from the Disney trip.

• One morning Joanne was making breakfast and thinking that she hadn't received a "41" in awhile. She opened a cupboard door to look for something. What she saw was a box of microwave popcorn on a higher shelf. The box was open, and the inside flaps were standing up. On the inside end flap was a giant #41.

• I did a guest appearance on a local cable show. Near the end of the show we began talking about the signs we were receiving from Nick, including white feathers. At the end of the show, as the credits were rolling, a small white feather slowly drifted down from the lights. The show's host asked in disbelief, "Is that a feather?"

It was, and we have it on tape.

• Joanne's biggest fear was that Nick may have suffered in the fire. She was thinking about this while driving one day. Just then, she saw the license plate of a car coming in the opposite direction. The plate read, "NOPAIN."

• Joe, Nick's grandfather, was driving down a country road, edged on both sides by long wire fences. There was someone walking up ahead. As Joe approached, he was really taken by how much this young man resembled Nick. The youth was wearing a denim jacket and had long blond hair. He was Nick's height and build. As he passed this young man, Joe wanted to get a better look. He started to pull over, looked into his rear-view mirror, and young man was gone.

• While Christmas shopping in a small gift boutique, Nick's grandmother, Barbara, noticed a collection of charming angel music boxes, high on a shelf. One angel caught her attention. It had billowy wings, flowing blond hair, and striking blue eyes. This angel reminded her of Nick. Barbara thought about buying it, then had second thoughts. As she turned to walk away, the beautiful music box began to play, all on its own.

The angel went home with Grandma.

• Christian DeRezendes had been thinking about producing an independent film telling the story of our "41" experiences. He made the final decision to produce his documentary *41 The Movie* after leaving his house one day to find a dumpster in his driveway with a giant 41 on the side.

These are just 41 examples of the incidents that take place every day. Believe me, I could give you 4100 more. But, if I did this book would be five inches thick and cost $1,495.

Besides, I may want to write a sequel.

-41-
To You and To You

First to *you*. Chances are that after reading this book or at least part of it, you've decided that I'm completely out of my tree. You don't believe or accept what I've written here. You may feel sorry for me and believe that I'm just a bereaved father who can't get over the loss of his son.

I understand your feelings and I thank you for your concern. But you're wrong.

If you've decided for yourself that your son, daughter, sister, mother, father, husband, lover or wife, are really gone, what do you have? Do you really want to continue to believe that you were supposed to have these people, love them, care for them and cherish the time you have with them, only to be punished with their sudden exit, never to see or hear from them again?

At every funeral I've ever attended, I have heard people say, "He (she) will never be forgotten."

Of course not! And I'll tell you why. *Because these people are not dead.* They are heart and soul. They are love and joy. They are laughter and tears. They are yours. And I'll tell you something else they are. They're still right here, right now.

I know that you want to believe that, but you're afraid. You're afraid that I am wrong. I'm not. You're afraid to be disappointed. You're afraid to be made a fool of. You won't be. This is not a child's myth, like Santa Claus or the Tooth Fairy.

This is real.

Understand this. It has never been my goal to convince you of anything. I couldn't if I wanted to. I've only told you what has happened and continues to happen to our family and friends everyday. The messages, signs and events I've told you about are real.

My message is that you too can experience these types of signs and communications. Oh, they may not be with the same frequency and strength Nick has been able to offer. But the signs are there. You just need to hear and see them.

Then next time you're in a supermarket and you hear a special song that connects you with a loved one who has passed, stop and listen. When you get a check from a waitress and it ends in your loved one's lucky number, acknowledge it. When you see a license plate that carries the name of someone who has passed, or an expression that reminds you of them, say "hello," if only to yourself.

There's an old phrase that refers to "hiding in plain sight." That is where you'll find the loved one you miss so much. All you need to do is open your eyes, open your mind and open your heart.

And now for *you*, I know that you believe what I've written is true, and you believe it because it's happened to you. You've had signs, messages and assurances that your loved one is still with you. I know how difficult it is to talk about these events. You want people to believe you, but you fear being looked upon as a nut. Well, I do believe you. I am so happy for you, and I want to help you tell others.

It's my goal to turn *41 Signs of Hope* into a series of books that will tell not only our story but your story and those of thousands of other people just like you and me. Remember, the more people know, the more they will be able to recognize their own signs and tell their own stories.

I want you to write to me and give me all the details of your sign, your visit or other "unexplained" occurrence. I will review it and consider putting it in another book, this time with *your* "Signs of Hope."

You can contact me online at www.41signsofhope.com. Click on the link: "Share your story of a loved one's survival." This will bring up a confidential form that you can fill out online and that will be e-mailed directly to me when you click the "submit" button. You also can contact me by regular mail via the publisher: Dave Kane, c/o New River Press, 645 Fairmount St., Woonsocket, RI 02895.

Contacts

The mediums and organizations mentioned in this book are available to render advice and help. Among them:

Cindy Gilman, Spiritual Medium
401-885-4115

Maureen Hancock, Spiritual Medium
www.maureenhancock.com

Robert Brown, Spiritual Medium
www.robertbrown-medium.com

The Forever Family Foundation
www.foreverfamilyfoundation.org

Roland Comtois, Spiritual Medium
www.rolandcomtoisjr.com

Acknowledgments

No one accomplishes anything of real value totally on their own. That is certainly true about the writing of this book. Nicky's friends and family, especially his brothers Chris, Billy and David, have all been instrumental, not only in their support but in their devotion in helping to tell his story.

They all share equally in this proud accomplishment, and I thank them sincerely.

The special contributions of Charlie Hall, Jon Land, Robert Brown and my publisher, Paul Eno, are truly appreciated.

Hi Vito!

The Author

Dave Kane is a prominent radio talk-show host in Rhode Island. He also performs as a stand-up comedian and has a one-man show called *Misgivings*. His other activities include running his own creative consulting company, Dave Kane Ideas.

41 Signs of Hope was inspired by the messages Dave and his family have received from his son Nicholas since his passing in The Station nightclub fire in Rhode Island in February 2003.

41 SIGNS of HOPE